QUESTIONS
teens are asking today

QUESTIONS
teens are asking today

Theodore W. Schroeder and Dean Nadasdy

Publishing House
St. Louis

© 1987 by Concordia Publishing House
3558 South Jefferson Avenue, St. Louis, MO 63118-3968.
Manufactured in the United States of America.

Library of Congress Cataloging-in-Publication Data

Schroeder, Ted W., 1939-
      Questions teens are asking.

      1. Youth—Conduct of life. 2. Youth—Religious life. I. Nadasdy, Dean, 1947- . II Title.
BJ1581.2.S392 1986   248.8'3   86-21537
ISBN 0-570-04454-5

---

1 2 3 4 5 6 7 8 9 10 MAL 95 94 93 92 91 90 89 88 87

*To the youth
of the parishes we have served
and to the students
at Minneapolis Lutheran High School*

Contents

Introduction

"Why do boys' bikes have a bar across and why don't girls' bikes?"

"Is it possible to think a thought that no one else has ever thought?"

"Does your brain weigh less when you forget something?"

"What is the most painless way to commit suicide?"

When I was a teen, questions like that used to run around in my head all the time. Partly because my world was changing so fast, and partly because I was noticing things I had never seen as a child, I was full of questions. Nothing seemed to make much sense. God seemed more and more distant, and people less and less dependable. The future looked like a fearsome giant, and the past bristled with the foolishness and failings that I'd just as soon have forgotten.

But the biggest trouble with all the questions was that I didn't know what to do with them. I wasn't sure whether anyone else thought about such questions, whether anyone cared if I did, or whether anyone could or would give me answers to the questions.

Not that my parents didn't listen. They'd answer questions all right. But they liked "sensible" questions—questions about what kind of clothes to wear, about religion, or about what was happening in the world. My most pressing questions, the ones that really bugged me, were often met with "Oh, that's silly!" or "What kind of a question is that?"

I had no way of telling what was a "good" question and what was a "silly" question. So I didn't ask most of them. I just wondered and got more and more confused.

Of course, some of my questions weren't answerable anyway. I don't suppose anyone knows yet why, if you press on your eyelids, you see funny colors, or why people who laugh loudly usually sneeze quietly. But it might have been good to have had someone listen to my questions anyway. It might have been helpful to have had someone at least try to answer them.

Part of the hurt of being a teen is the feeling that you just aren't quite put together right. Somehow you are built wrong, or your head works wrong, or you do things wrong—at least, you don't feel quite "all there." And it's so hard to find out if you really are a total reject or if those feelings are just more of those odd questions that run around in your head.

This little book certainly doesn't pretend to answer all the hard questions that teens can think up. It doesn't even take on some of the tougher ones. But it does try to let teens know that their questions are important and that they deserve an answer—even if that answer doesn't make the question go away completely.

Teens won't find answers here to the great philosophical questions that have troubled people for ages. We have no idea, for example, why God made the world in the first place. But we'd like to offer direct and honest responses to questions that might be troubling teens—questions about people, about relationships, and about why people do what they do.

Certainly, the answers a teen will find here are not definitive. We have made no attempt to document our conclusions or to do research to establish that what we say is a fact.

But we do try to respond, to answer with love and concern and respect—to answer as we might answer if the question came from a real teen, right here with us, sitting on his or her hands, stumbling a little on the words.

As we have written these answers, we have tried to make sure that the questioner feels that we have heard and understood the question and that we know why that question is important; we have made an attempt to offer the best answer we know; and we have made a point to bring in the Word and especially the Good News of God's salvation in Jesus Christ as the "best" answer to every question.

Some teens won't like our answers very much; others will feel that we have avoided the questions that still bother them. For those who struggle with questions and have no one to listen, for those who wonder and can't find anyone who seems to care, and for those who still aren't sure whether their questions are "silly" or not—this book of questions and answers may help. By God's grace it may move a wondering teen past the place where the world looks like a mysterious jumble of senseless happenings to that place where some things, at least, start to fit together—where the world starts to have meaning, where life begins to have purpose.

That is our hope and our prayer as teens read these questions and answers. The questions are all "real" questions. We did not make them up. They came from teens—many of them from the students at Minneapolis Lutheran High School. Others are from teens we have known, loved, talked to, counseled, listened to, and shared with.

We pray that those who read this will be "touched" by the Comforter—the Spirit; that He will renew and enlighten each questioner—not necessarily with all the answers, but with the assurance that even those who muddle through with too many questions and not enough answers are loved by God in Jesus Christ.

What better answer is there than that?

Q *Why doesn't my dad love me?*

A He probably does. Most fathers care a great deal about their children. A father may pretend he doesn't know much about how to take care of his child—"all thumbs, you know"; he will probably duck out on the feeding and diapering or pretend that he's not very good at playing or pretending. But he'll probably cherish his child in a special way. He'll see in his son or daughter a reflection of himself, a remembrance of his own childhood. And he'll dream of helping his child do some of the things he never had a chance to do or be some of the things he could never be. His secret hopes and dreams will be tied up in that child, hopes and dreams that may even drive him to be a better, richer, or more successful father than all the rest.

So, without a doubt, your father does love you. The real question may be—why can't my father show me that he loves me? The reasons are many.

It may just be that your father is disappointed in you. He may see in you many of the weaknesses and faults that he himself struggles with. You may put things off like he does—and he wishes you weren't that way. You may have the same short fuse he has, or be as messy as he is, or tend to forget things like he does. And when he sees those failings in you, he becomes angry—not so much at you, but at himself. He may find it hard then to show you affection or approval because he does not want to give the impression that he approves of the very faults that have haunted his life.

Another reason your father may seem distant is that he may think he is helping you by being demanding and severe. Your father may see the coldness of the world, the difficult choices he has had to make, the pain he has suffered at the hands of others. And he may simply feel that he is preparing you for what you will find in life by treating you just a little like you may be treated out there. "Life is tough," he may say or think. "No one is going to hand my kid a ticket to easy street. He might as well get used to that right now." Of course, what you may need to survive the hard knocks you will experience out there is a little love, acceptance, and support—but parents don't always see things the same way you do. If you suspect that your father is leaning on you in order to "toughen" you, you might try talking to him about it. He just may decide that toughness training may not be the best way to help you at this point in your life.

Another major reason fathers often find themselves paralyzed when it comes to showing love is that in our culture it is not considered "manly" (whatever that is) to be affectionate. Somehow showing affection (touching someone, giving a hug, kissing, etc.) is thought to be "feminine"—something girls do. That attitude is so strong that men are often suspected of being gay if they show too much tenderness, too much emotion, or too much feeling for others. Young men who are naturally very sensitive—who experience strong feelings toward others and desire to show those feelings—are quickly teased and shamed into being "macho"—tough and strong and "cool."

Strangely, it may be true that while you are sitting in your room wondering why your father does not care, your father is wondering how he can show that he cares without seeming weak or silly. He may have lived the macho image so long that it is almost impossible for him to do anything else now.

Oh, he'll show you he loves you. He'll give you orders for your own good. He'll check out how you take care of things around the house. He'll even get you a gift once in a while—something you might need in the future. But he'll probably find it very hard to hug you or kiss you—if you are a boy, because grown men don't kiss other grown men, and if you are a girl, because "good" fathers don't touch their grown daughters lest their touch be misunderstood. He may find it almost impossible to say "I love you." He may have found it almost impossible to say those very words to your mother, even many years ago when he was thinking of walking down the aisle with her.

And it may be that you won't be able to change him much. You may not be able to get him to show you the kind of affection you need from him. You may have to accept the indirect ways he has of paying attention to you, even when that attention is not very pleasant.

14

But you can show your love to him. Let him know that you care. You don't have to get slobbery about it. You don't even have to go out of your way. Just put in a word or a touch here and there that lets him know that you think he's important and that you care about him. He may not know what to do about it when you tell him that you love him. He may not be able to respond very well. But it will get through to him. It will make a difference for him. And who knows? Maybe he'll get the hint and give you a hug back once in a while.

Here are some other things you can do to make a change in the relationship between you and your dad:

1. Pray for him. You may not know the pressures, the problems, the difficulties he is dealing with every day. He may not be able to tell you about them. He may be struggling with hurts you cannot even imagine. He may be frightened because he can see himself getting older and cannot stop the changes that age brings. He may be frustrated because he cannot make the money or achieve the success he would like. He may be tired of trying, unable to cope, longing for something special in his life. He may feel unwanted and unappreciated. All of those hurts and worries may be going around in his head—all of them causing him to appear to be caught up in himself and less interested in you. Pray for him. Ask God to give him wisdom, peace, contentment, and a feeling of security. And, most of all, ask God to give him the assurance that he is a loved child of God, no matter what is going right or wrong in his life.

2. Forgive him even when he doesn't ask for it. The Good News of God's love for us in Jesus is that He comes to us and forgives us, even when we're not ready, even when we keep on making the same mistakes, even when we're not very lovable or forgivable. Still He loves. Still He forgives. Still He reaches out and assures us of His eternal love because of Jesus. Perhaps as we respond to God with thanks for that great love, we can look for His help to show some of that unexpected, unconditional love to our sometimes-less-than-perfect father.

3. Talk to him. The talks may not always amount to much. He may be impatient. He may appear to have other things on his mind. He may end up giving you a lecture again. But don't

give up. Your ability to talk to one another, to exchange ideas, to hear each other, to share your feelings is at the very core of your relationship. It may not be easy to get real talk underway. But it will be worth more than a passing effort.

4. Talk to someone else about your dad. Start with your mother, perhaps, or your pastor, or someone who knows him well. Don't just complain. It's not necessary to go into a long explanation of what you think is wrong with your father. But ask that other person to help you understand your dad better. Very likely they have insights into your dad that you cannot have.

Listen to what they say about him. Try to use their eyes to see your dad in a different way—to see what is going on in his life and what makes him act the way he does. It may make a lot of difference in what you expect of your dad and what you are willing to do for him.

Love is pretty wonderful stuff. You can't really study it very well; and it's hard to label it or discover just what it is like or how people experience it. But it is powerful. Given away, it makes the person who gives it and the person who receives it richer. And most of the time when it is given, it comes back in greater measure than it was sent out.

Want to know how much your dad loves you? Try sending him your love and see what comes back.

Q *Why are my parents never satisfied? No matter what I do—how hard I try—they're still on my case. All I ever hear is nag, nag, about what I should have done better or what I should not have done. They never ever tell me I did a good job. Everything I do is always wrong. Why?*

A I once knew a guy who had probably the most remarkably ordinary dog in the world. The only thing special about his dog was that he was so totally unspecial. The dog was a plain old mutt with plain brown fur and plain off-white spots. The dog seemed to move around all right, but he was obviously neither smarter nor more talented than a million other dogs. But his owner was convinced that this "reluctant Rover" was none other than "superdog" in the flesh. He boasted about his dog constantly. You could see him out in the yard trying to teach the poor pooch to jump through a hoop, or to heel, or to do some other stunt he'd seen some wonder dog do. I remember one time he spent about a month throwing a frisbee at the poor hound. I don't think that dog ever caught the thing. He got so he could run and get it all right, but he never could follow it in the air or grab it as it went by. But my friend was undaunted. "This is such a wonderful dog!" he'd say to anyone who'd listen. "He's getting ready to learn tricks no dog ever did before."

Obviously, the dog was about as close to being superdog as most of us are to being superperson. But the owner thought he was super because he loved that dog. Surely, that dog must look as out of the ordinary, as lovable, and as capable to everyone else as he did to him! After all, he cherished that dog—and that fact alone ought to make the dog able to do all the things he hoped or dreamed his dog could do.

Something like that happens to parents. Oh, they don't mean it to. They can even see how other people do exactly what the guy with the dog did. They can see how the other parents think their kid is the brightest, the smartest, and the most able. They notice how those other parents push their kid to be the best, to do the best. They see how all of them think their kid has to have the lead in the play, to be the head cheerleader, to be the quarterback on the team, to be the honor scholar of the district. Obviously, they think their kid is the best because he or she is their kid.

And even though they can see this trait in others, they still act the same way themselves, because, of course, in their case they are not pushing their child to be anything he or she can't be. They are, of course, only being realistic about his or her remarkable athletic, scholastic, or dramatic talents. And, of course, they owe it to the school, to the coaches, and to the teachers to point out how overlooking their child would be a grave error. Why, certainly, in that oversight the best and most talented would miss the part, the grade, or the place on the team that their child should have.

Well, all of that may not be so bad—I mean, no one minds being told he or she is the best and most talented. We all like to be fussed over and complimented. But the problem is that the superteen that your folks may have created may not be anything like you at all. The superteen who inhabits their imagination may have your name, but he may have almost nothing else in common with you. He may be smarter and more athletic than you. He may be neater, more mannerly, more loving, and more appreciative—and all the other things that your folks think you ought to be or to do. And since you are not yet much like superteen, they think that the best way to get you there is to point out to you how you have not yet arrived. If you are not the neatest kid on the block, obviously they ought to let you know the area of improvement you ought to pay attention to. Similarly, if your grades are not quite up there where people are going to be looking to putting your name in the paper, then surely they can help you by telling you how you could study more so that your grades would be better. And so it goes. They are telling you how to dress, how to talk, how to eat, how to stand, how to sleep, work, and so on—all for your own good so that one day you just might sneak up there and get to be superteen, an accomplishment your folks could rightly take credit for.

And this is not to put down parents. Many parents suffer from the superteen problem. It comes with the job. Parents want what's best for their children. They want them to have an easy go of it out there in the world. They want them to be looked up to, to be successful, to be accomplished, and to be respected. And they consider it their duty to try to make that happen.

Unfortunately, all of this instructing, guiding, teaching, and telling comes across as criticism. It comes across as faultfinding. It comes across as blaming, accusing, attacking, and putting down. In short, it is just plain painful to be told all the time where you are lacking, where you are not up to what you should be, and where you are at fault. That pain can make you feel bad about yourself, angry at your parents, frustrated about what you have to do, and depressed about where you are in your life and generally make you want to get away somehow or other.

Also, unfortunately, it is probably not going to be possible for you to get your folks to throw superteen in the trash can and just like you for who you are. They would see that as a failure of their responsibility as parents. They really think that they are helping you become the best you can be. And that's what parents are for, isn't it?

Maybe the best thing you can do is to understand where they are coming from. Certainly, they don't mean to hurt you or run you down. They don't mean to make your life harder. Most assuredly they don't want to make things more painful for you. For better or for worse, they are trying to help. Maybe the most important thing you can do is to hear what they are saying not so much as criticism but as an attempt (perhaps not a very good one) to help.

Q *Why does my friend get so angry when I go around with other kids? I'm not hurting her. She acts as if she owns me or something.*

A Watch a young child with a new toy—say a four-year-old with a brand-new, genuine, "ruff and ready" dump truck. Watch him around other children. He will be delighted if the others watch him play with his new truck, admire his new truck, even touch his new truck. But they'd better not try to take his truck or play with it when he's not looking. "Mine!" he will say as loudly as possible at the first move anyone makes to latch onto his truck. "It's *mine,* and you can't play with it!"

It's not that he wants to be selfish—he certainly doesn't think through what his actions might mean for his future. It may well be that the other children will learn to avoid him and refuse to share their toys with him. But the lure of the new truck is too great—the need to keep it, to control it—not only because it is fun to play with but because of the status it gives him among the others. As a result, he cannot part with it, even for an instant. It's his truck—and everyone will know it, everyone will appreciate it, and everyone will live with it, like it or not.

When people get to their teens, they no longer defend toys with their life. They no longer grasp at playthings and try to gain status by having the brightest and best toy truck. But the feelings don't change. The need for approval, the need to be important, the need to be noticed, and the need to be in control doesn't change. It just shows itself in different ways.

Certainly, even for teens, there is status in having the best stuff—in being admired for having the best clothing, the most outrageous hairdo, the neatest car, and so on. There is a certain feeling of "specialness" in being the most admired, the most envied, or the "luckiest" person. That feeling of being unique, special, or looked up to loses very little of its desirability between one's 4th and 18th year. And it makes us do very strange things, like trying to own people.

Even though we know logically that we cannot own others, that we cannot control them, and that we can barely influence

21

them, there is a part of us that wants to say *"mine!"* when it comes to an admired and important friend. If we have a friend who is looked up to by others, a person who is recognized as beautiful or important or smart—whatever—just being around that person makes us look better. And if we can say that person is our "best friend," then we really have it made. Obviously, that important person would not be best friends with a jerk or with a reject. And even though we might feel like a reject on occasion, knowing that we are important enough to have a best friend whom people envy is almost like being four years old again with the newest and brightest and best red truck in the whole neighborhood.

The need to appear important by attaching oneself to someone important becomes especially critical to the person who feels terribly unimportant. Think of the teens who hold on to their friends too tightly, try to control them, and try to keep others away from them. Think of those who almost make fools of themselves because of their jealousy, their demands, and their plotting always to be closest to the people they admire. They are the ones who hurt inside. They are the ones who have convinced themselves that they are worthless, useless—they are sure they are rejects and can only be looked up to as special if they are attached to some other obviously special person.

It's not that they want to be selfish. They don't even analyze the implications of their jealousy or their need to control. They don't seem to see that their demands on their friends will probably eventually drive them away. They don't seem to understand that real friendship is giving, loving, accepting, and being happy with another person when that person is happy; real friendship is making that other person feel cared about, no matter what he or she does.

"Friends" who try to control, who get jealous over the time you spend with others, who test you to see if you really care about them, or who want you to be with them all the time are acting out of the fear that they will be alone, and that they will seem as rejected to others as they do to themselves. And they can't stand it. They can't take the chance. They can't live with being the weirdest reject in the class. And so they work very hard to prevent that from happening—and by their work, they often make it happen. They become the reject they are trying not to be. People stay away because they do not want to be controlled, do not want to be owned, and do not want to be pushed around by someone else.

It's pretty hard to like a person who dislikes himself or herself. All of us dislike ourselves sometimes. When we blow the chemistry test for the third time, when we fall down the front stairs right in front of everybody, or when we sit there like a dope when the teacher asks a question, we aren't too crazy about ourselves. At that point we probably dislike ourselves, wish we were someone else, wish we could change, or wish we could start over again. But for most of us that feeling passes. When something good happens—when the right girl likes us, or the right guy pays attention to us—we feel pretty good about ourselves; we like ourselves again. But for some people the change to liking themselves never comes. They are always down on themselves, always feeling terrible inside, always on the verge of hating themselves. And those who don't like themselves don't really understand how anyone else could like them either. They are suspicious of those who seem to care. They don't really believe it when someone wants to be their friend. They just can't accept the genuine friendship of another person, especially a person they admire.

But they need a friend. A person who hates himself may only have you to let him know that he is not a reject. The friend who dislikes herself may have only you to keep her from giving up on herself and doing something really stupid like using drugs or running away or worse.

But it won't be easy. You'll have to overlook a lot when you are a friend to a self-hater. You'll have to ignore it when that person tries to plan your life for you, monopolizes your time, comes down on you for failing to pay attention to her, or cries over the times you seem too interested in someone else. You'll have to put up with her jealousy, anger, demands, and attempts to control. But if you can, you will be accomplishing something pretty important with your friendship. You'll be helping a hurting person learn to love herself, and that is a very special thing to do.

That person, more than any other you might meet, needs to know how much God loves her, needs to know that God made her special, needs to know that God cares, needs to know that she is so important to God that He would give His own Son for her. She needs to know that no matter what she has done, she is forgiven and safe in Jesus Christ.

And you might be able to help get that message across. That won't be easy either. A sermon won't do it. She won't believe you. Arguing won't do it—feelings of self-hate have nothing to do with the evidence. But loving that person can make a difference. Being there can help. Showing you care can start to change that hatred to at least self-acceptance. And it just may be that in all the faces that pass by, all those who turn away, all those who reject, all those who couldn't care less—your caring can make it possible for that hurting person to begin to understand the love that God has for her—not because you say you care but because you do your caring.

There's a lot to be said for getting the word out about Jesus as Savior to those who have never heard. Certainly, it's important to witness to those who don't know Him. But in this case, for the friend who hurts with self-hatred, it might be the most important thing you do to let her see the love of Christ that comes to you and through you to her.

Why are parents more protective as their child nears graduation?

 As they say, it's a cold, cruel world out there. It really is. Your parents probably know firsthand some of the hard knocks the world has to offer.

People are pretty mean out there. They'll stab you in the back just to get ahead of you. Some people are really strange. What they do doesn't even make any sense. Others are downright dangerous. There are those who will take from you, take advantage of you, cheat you, hurt you, even kill you without a thought.

And things can get pretty muddled and confusing out there. The decisions you have to make when a boss tells you to cheat on an order, when a friend "lets you in on a little quick money," or when someone wants you to go along with the latest "entertainment" are all pretty hard. People keep pressing you to change your life-style, forget your values, and get away from "old-fashioned" ways of doing things. And just about the time you think you have a real friend, she turns on you, makes a fool of you, or takes advantage of you. Even worse, just about the time you think you've found the one who will really love you, he leaves you, runs off with some airhead, and forgets all the promises he ever made to you. And what can you do then but cry?

It is a hard world out there. That's not just talk from a lot of worried adults and overprotective parents. The one thing you can be sure of when you leave the "safety" of your parents' house is that you will get hurt; you will get in over your head; you will be lonely sometimes, frightened sometimes, and confused sometimes.

But that may still not seem like a big deal to you. You may already know about how people are, about how they pressure you to do and be what you don't want to do and be. You may have already been disappointed in others lots of times and come through some really rough deals more times than you can count. So, you might ask, what's a little more of the same? What's the problem? You know what's happening. You know what's going on. What's all the fuss about?

Well, the problem is that your parents don't think you're

ready. They have not had time to adjust to the fact that you have changed from a helpless child who couldn't even feed yourself to a competent and relatively self-sufficient adult. After all, they didn't have much time to get used to the idea. It seems to them that all of a sudden you are grown. They don't even know how it happened—the time got away so quickly.

And they think of all the things they should have done to get you ready for what might happen to you when you leave home. They should have taught you more about living and loving, sewing and cooking, fixing and fending, and taking care of the car. They should have warned you more and informed you more. They should have given you more of their time and paid more attention to you. Very likely they are feeling guilty because of what they did not do for you as you were growing.

And, of course, they see your faults pretty well. After all, they have most of the same faults themselves. They may worry that you are too trusting, too gullible. They may be frightened by the fact that you don't seem to be a very good self-starter, that you take a lot of time to make up your mind, and that you don't seem to pay a lot of attention to what's happening around you. They may see weaknesses in you that you aren't even aware of. And they think about them—late at night when they lie awake—and they worry about the time when you will go off on your own to college, to a new job, even to marriage.

"She's not ready!" says a very loud voice inside their heads. "She'll never make it!" And, of course, the way they deal with that fearful little voice is to try to get in lots of last-minute instructions and lots of almost-too-late protection. So the older you get, the more they seem to treat you like a child, the more they seem to tell you things you already know, and the more they try to isolate you from or insulate you against the cold, cruel world.

But they mean it for the best. If they didn't care, they wouldn't bother. If they wanted to get rid of you, they'd let go so fast you'd find yourself outside the front door before you even had time to pack your bag. At least they care. And they want to help you be ready to deal with what may be waiting for you in the world that they know, that they have lived through, and that they sometimes fear.

26

How can I keep from getting mad at people? It seems like I'm always flying off the handle about something. I get angry so easily.

 Well, first of all, it probably won't be possible for you to keep from *getting* angry. Anger is an emotion. It is a feeling that happens to us—in us. We don't decide to be angry anymore than we decide to be happy. It happens. We can sometimes control the things that make feelings happen, but we don't really control the feelings. For example, if we know that a certain person always aggravates us, we can avoid him. But we can't keep from being aggravated once we're dealing with him.

Some people seem to get angry more easily than others. Maybe you're one of those. Maybe they say quietly behind your back, "He has a short fuse." Doctors would probably say that you have a "limited tolerance for frustration." Whatever you call it— for some reason that is built into you, you get angry quickly— maybe too quickly for your own good.

The thing to remember is that anger in itself is not always wrong. In itself, it is no more wrong to be angry than it is to be sad or to be glad. The Bible tells us that God was angry many times. Jesus was apparently angry when He drove the money-changers from the temple. And the Bible tells us to "be angry, but don't sin" (Eph. 4:26). So, while it is in itself not wrong to be angry, anger is dangerous in that it pushes us to think and do things that are wrong, that we might later be sorry for.

When I am angry with someone who has hurt me, anger says, "Go ahead. Get back at her. She deserves it, and you'll feel better." The trouble is that at that moment what anger is saying is at least partly true. There is a certain instant "reward" in getting back at the person who has done you wrong. It feels kind of good to insult the one who has insulted you, to yell at the one who yelled at you, even to hit the one who first hit you. Not only does it show that person that you are not an easy mark, but it lets the person feel a "little of his or her own medicine."

The "good feeling" that revenge offers passes quickly. Pretty soon we begin to realize how foolish we must have seemed when we were hitting back like a two-year-old, how dumb we must have looked yelling like that, and how sad we are going to feel when the person we got back at will never speak to us again. So anger quickly gets us into trouble. It moves us to strike out, to hurt, to make another person feel some of the hurt we are feeling. And when we do that, we are not only wrong but are likely to do damage that will take a long time to heal.

Anger is funny stuff. Research shows that if we "let it all hang out" when we are angry, instead of making the anger better, it makes it worse. When we let anger control us—make us shout and say things to hurt, strike out and do things to hurt—it only makes anger more at home in us and makes us more likely to do the same the next time we are angry.

Anger, like other strong and sometimes destructive emotions, needs to be understood, confronted, and, with God's help, controlled.

Oh, it won't be easy. Controlling emotions is never easy, like when you're in the pits—really feeling depressed, really bumming. You can tell yourself a hundred times you should be feeling better. You can even listen to someone else tell you how you have so much to be thankful for and happy about. But it doesn't help a bit. In fact, it can make the whole thing worse because you start to feel guilty about being depressed and that makes you feel even more depressed. It's possible to turn depression around, but it takes time, support, and encouragement from others, and some careful attention to our thoughts and needs before it begins to go away.

Anger is no easier than depression to control—in fact, it's harder. Depression is tough to take, but at least it's slow and quiet. Anger is hot and fiery—quick to take over and always trying to make us do wrong.

You will want to do some things that might help you deal with your anger in a more helpful way:

1. Learn which people are likely to make you angry and do your best to avoid them. Sure, our Christian faith tells us that we should love everyone. But it may not be possible to *like* everyone, to enjoy everyone's company, and to get along easily with everyone. Some people may do things that simply drive us

crazy. So we may have to avoid the guy who bugs us, the one who always asks favors, and the one who makes demands.

2. Learn what situations are likely to make you angry, and do your best to avoid those, too. Being overtired, being under a great deal of stress, or being anxious about something we have to do can make our "fuse" shorter. In fact, any "pressure" we put on ourselves physically can make us lose emotional control more quickly. When we are under stress, when we are over-tired, or when we are run down because we haven't eaten much in a long time, we're just plain on edge. And it doesn't take much to fall into anger when we are already "on the edge." Keeping active, eating right, getting enough sleep, and managing the pressures to get things done are part of learning to control our temper.

3. Be honest and admit to friends and family that you indeed do have a short fuse and that you will probably get angry some-times—even when you don't mean to. Ask them to be patient with you, to try to understand, and to forgive you for becom-ing angry and saying what you don't mean. Tell them that you will try to let them know when you are feeling particularly "un-ready" to deal with your anger—when you're down, when you're under pressure, or when you're in a hurry. Ask them to give you a little more room then so that you will not find your-self flying off the handle. Then do the same for them.

4. Find "safe" ways to get rid of your anger. It is not all right to beat up on someone when you are angry. But there is nothing wrong with jabbing a punching bag or beating your feet on the street as you jog. There's nothing wrong with hitting the day-lights out of a tennis ball or golf ball or driving to the basket in a pick-up game. Regular physical activity is a good way to get the anger out without doing damage or making a fool of yourself.

5. Take your problem honestly to God for His help, support, and forgiveness. The great thing about our God is that He's not a distant watcher—One off there in space somewhere who kind of keeps an eye on us through a spiritual telescope, blaming us for our weaknesses and overlooking our faults. Our God is in-volved in life with us. Jesus Himself dealt with all the tempta-

30

tions that bug you. He too had to live with temptations to act in anger—because He was human. Though He did not sin as He experienced anger, He surely knows and understands what you are going through when you are angry. For that reason you can tell Him about your anger and know that He will hear and understand. You can ask Him to help you deal with the anger in a way that won't hurt others and won't hurt you either. And, most important, you can ask Him to forgive you when the anger does get the best of you and you do something that you didn't mean to. You can be sure that He will forgive you, set you right again, put the angry actions away, and let you start over again as though that mistake, that sin, never happened.

Knowing that God has forgiven you can give you the strength to go to the person you have attacked, insulted, or hurt and ask him or her to forgive you, too. When that is done, anger has been beaten once more. It has been beaten not because you were able to change yourself, or pretend that anger doesn't happen, or change your emotions—those are pretty impossible things to do. It's been beaten because the results of that anger, what it can do to you and what it can do to the person who is on the other end of the anger, have been healed again by God's power in Jesus Christ. Anger has been made powerless because it cannot destroy anything—and that is what defeats it.

One last word: the worst thing we can do with anger is save it. It's like keeping the garbage in the house after it has started to rot. It's like leaving the splinter in your finger after it has started to fester. Saved anger is absolutely destructive. It destroys relationships, makes you unable to deal with other situations that make you angry, gets worse as it is saved, and eventually will move you to destructive actions. Saved anger—the anger that we hold against someone when we say to ourselves, "I'll never forgive her for what she did"—is like a bomb with a lit fuse. It gets hotter and hotter and more and more dangerous until there is an explosion, and someone is invariably hurt.

Whatever we do about situations that make us angry and about trying to avoid those who get to us, the most important thing we can ask God to do is to help us get rid of saved anger.

We need His help to overcome the hurt done to us, to look past it, and to love the one who has hurt us in spite of that hurt—a little like the way He has loved us. Forgiving, though not easy, is the way the saved anger is put away—forever.

Why is it so hard to do what's right?

 A guy I know answers all *why* questions about people the same way. It doesn't make any difference if the question is "Why are there so many divorces?" or "Why do kids suck their thumbs?" The answer is always the same. "It's because of sin," he says.

His answer may seem a little too simple—even a little silly. But he has a point. Most things that cause us to ask why are because of sin. People's sinfulness lies at the heart of all human failing, weakness, sickness, even death.

"Why is it so hard to do right?" Because of sin.

Certainly, that's true. It is the sin in us, the desire to go our own way, the need to "do our own thing," the illusion that we can be our own boss and take care of our own life that makes it so hard to do right.

St. Paul calls the sinner in us our "old man" (Rom. 6:6 KJV; cf. Eph. 4:22) or our "sinful self." Whatever we call it, we all have in us a strong desire to break the rules, to take what we can, to make ourselves our own god, to take advantage of others, and to serve ourselves. It doesn't make much difference how much we think about getting rid of that sinner; it doesn't matter how many good intentions we have about "doing the right thing" in spite of him; he'll often get the upper hand, and we'll find ourselves breaking the rules again, hurting someone again, and running away from God again.

That's the bad news—the sinner in us is still there, still strong. Even though we've been baptized, even though we are God's children and are forgiven, even though He gives us His Spirit to help us—the sinner is still alive and well in us, and he must be dealt with constantly.

But the good news is that for us at least there is a battle. For many people the war is over. They have given up and given in to the sinner. They no longer even try to do what is right and to avoid what is evil. They never even think about the will of God or worry about the needs and wants of others. They run roughshod

33

over people, over life—over everything. You know them. They are those who seem to have no conscience. They fairly bristle with self-importance. Often you can sense danger when you are around them. It is evident from their style, their actions, and their speech that they care for no one but themselves and will do anything to anyone to get where they think they want to be.

There is no more battle for them. They simply live as fast as they can until they die. There is no "good against evil" battle. For them, good has already lost.

We have a sense about what God wants us to be and to do. We know what He has told us is His will, and a part of us (Martin Luther calls it the "saint" in us) wants to obey God's will—to love others, to help those in need, to serve those who are helpless, and to reach out with the Word to those who are lost. A part of us wants to care about our neighbor and live a life of worshipful recognition of Jesus' lordship over our lives.

And the saint has his way—sometimes anyway. Sometimes the Spirit helps us, and we are able to do something for someone else with absolutely no expectation of a reward. Sometimes we are able to point someone to the love of God in Christ without doing it simply out of a sense of duty. Sometimes our praise of God comes from a joyful heart and not out of habit. The saint is alive and well. The part of us that has been redeemed and made right by the death and resurrection of Jesus, the part of us that has been washed clean in Baptism and claimed by God is alive and well and at work by the Spirit's power.

It would be nice if we could finish off the sinner once and for all. It would be great if we could do him in and be free of the desire to break the will of God, be free from the need to do our own thing, to take instead of give, to use others instead of loving them. But he is not so easily done in. Even St. Paul, who dedicated his life to spreading the Gospel of Jesus Christ, said: "For I know that nothing good dwells within me, that is, in my flesh. I can will what is right, but I cannot do it. For I do not do the good I want, but the evil I do not want is what I do" (Rom. 7:18—19). That's why God's daily forgiveness is so important. It's pretty easy just to get used to being pushed around by our sinner. It's easy to fall into habits of selfishness and sin that very quickly become a way of life away from God. And if we don't think we have enough of a desire in ourselves to get into the habit of sinning, there are always all the others out there, who consider any attempt to live a life of loving service absolute foolishness, to push us in the direction of the sinner.

That sinner has to be done away with ("drowned," says Luther) by a daily trip to the cross of Christ where we receive once again the forgiveness we so obviously don't deserve, but that He has so effectively gotten for us. There the sinner's deeds of the past are forgiven and that "old man" is drowned once more in the grace and love of God, and we are set free to live our life of love and service to Him.

It's not easy to be a follower of the Savior. It means living a constant battle between the saint, who is owned by God and powered by the Spirit, and the sinner in us, who wants us to be as far from God as possible and as in control of our own destiny as we think we can be. The war goes on. It is with us every time we have to make a decision about the rightness or wrongness of an act or a thought, every time we are asked for help, every time we want to take something as our own, and every time we are tempted to step on someone else in order to get ahead. Dozens of times we are caught up in the fight. We might even get a little tired of fighting and struggling. We might get weary of trying to do right when no one else even seems to care. It might get to be a real burden to be the only one who even cares about right and wrong when everyone is going to the next "fun time" someone has devised. It may seem like a lot of effort—until we consider the alternative.

Here are some things to do to "get the upper hand" in the battle:

1. Go to the Word. God promises to send His Spirit to work in us through the Word. We don't get God's help by wishing or dreaming of it. He comes to us through the Word. Studying the Word, hearing the Word, and receiving the "Word" in the Sacrament are all ways in which God helps us in the battle against the sinner in us.

2. Support another sinner. As you encourage the other person, remind him of God's love in Jesus Christ, call him back when

he falls, rejoice with him over the good things the Spirit has worked through him—you will be encouraging yourself, too, and will be built up by the power of the Spirit.

3. Seek the Spirit's power to renew your worship and devotional life. When we pray, we open ourselves to the work of the Spirit; when we worship, we focus on God as the center of our lives; when we come to Him for forgiveness, we receive strength to renew the battle and claim the victory.

The battle won't get easier as the years go by. The things that the sinner wants us to do might change, the temptations that lie in wait for us might be different as we get older, but the sinner will still be there. He'll still be calling us to leave God and His will and to go our own way, to trade good for evil, and to exchange life for death.

But in the end we win. The best news is the last news. We can't lose, no matter how the battle rages, how often we fall, how tough it gets, how difficult the way, and how many times the sinner seems to overtake us. It doesn't matter if the sinner lines up all evil against us. We can't lose, for we can be sure that "neither death, nor life, nor angels, nor principalities, nor things present, nor things to come, nor powers, nor height, nor depth, nor anything else in all creation will be able to separate us from the love of God in Christ Jesus our Lord" (Rom. 8:38—39). "Thanks be to God, who gives us the victory through our Lord Jesus Christ" (1 Cor. 15:57). That's good news we can cherish every morning, hang onto for the rest of the day, write on our hearts, and hold in our minds just before we give the sinner his daily drowning in the grace of God.

Q *Why am I so stupid? Why can't I be smarter—like other people?*

A I used to ask the same question. My older sister was the absolute spelling champion of the whole school. She could spell anything. I even heard her spell *rheumatoid* once. (I just looked it up to make sure I got it right here.) I had trouble spelling words like *does* (is it *does* or *dose?*) and *tomorrow* (how many m's and r's?) and sometimes even my name. I thought I surely must be the most stupid kid in the whole school or maybe the whole country. How could anyone be so dumb that he couldn't tell if the word was *lose* or *loose?*

I used to pay a lot of attention to my bad spelling. I'd try to be sure I never had to write something anyone else would read. I'd have this sudden attack of teacher-I-have-to-leave-the-room whenever we had a spelling bee. I even made my handwriting as sloppy as possible so people couldn't tell if I was spelling the words right or not.

The problem was, I paid so much attention to how badly I spelled, I forgot all the other things I could do pretty well. I could read and understand things very quickly. I could speak easily. I had a great imagination. I even threw a baseball pretty well. But all these seemed like nothing compared to my terrible spelling.

There are a few people who are genuinely good at a number of things. They seem to shine at whatever they try to do. But these "super" people are pretty rare. Most people are good at some things and not very good at others. The best mechanic I know can't read or write very well. A musician I grew up with could play the piano better than almost anyone else, but he was always falling over his own feet.

Your question shows that by some standard you feel less able than most others. Very likely that feeling has to do with the things you have to do in school. Somehow in our society we have assumed that those who are able to do well on tests (especially the kinds of tests that teachers like to give) are intelligent. Everyone else is "stupid." It's not so.

Certainly, those who can easily remember facts, pass tests,

37

and answer essay questions have an easier time of it in school. But school tests are not tests of your intelligence and ability—certainly not of your worth as a person. School-type tests "fit" people with certain kinds of intelligence and give good grades to those who have the ability to remember the information that the tests require. But they rarely test personality, creativity, athletic skill, judgment, wisdom, sensitivity to others, perception, insight, the ability to solve a problem, the ability to influence others, the ability to judge or comprehend spatial relationships, muscular coordination, the ability to make comparisons and to see differences, and dozens of other kinds of talents and intelligence. You are very likely good at several of those—and they seldom show up on a test.

I have a friend who was often told she was "dumb." She never did well in school. She used to get Ds on tests, even when she studied very hard. She remembers school as painful and tries to avoid being compared to other people—even stays away from things like Bible classes so that people won't have a chance to make her look foolish. For years she thought of herself as "stupid" because she did poorly on tests, because other people told her she was "slow," and because teachers generally gave her poor grades—even though she put a lot of effort into her schoolwork.

But this same person has a kind of intelligence that is quite rare and remarkable. She has the ability to know what people are feeling—"where they are" and what is troubling them—instinctively, without any effort. She can do what those who call themselves counselors or psychologists spend years learning to do. She knows when someone hurts and often can understand the cause of that hurt, even without asking questions or using a lot of words. But she never got a grade for that kind of intelligence in school. She never got an A in sensitivity on her high school or college report card. Even though she has an ability that makes her special, out of the ordinary, and particularly valuable to those who need help—she never got an award, a trophy, a scholarship, or any recognition for her talent. In school she was ignored or put down, even though her talent is of much more benefit to others and to

society as a whole than the ability to memorize the names of vertebrate animals in biology or the symbols of the elements in chemistry.

The very worst thing you can do when you find that you are not as able as others in a certain area is to get down on yourself about everything. Who said you were dumb? Who has a right to say you are stupid?

God made you special. He gave you talents and abilities that others may not even come close to. He calls you His own; He bought you with His own Son because He loves you; He forgives you and holds you in the palm of His hand—not because you can or can't get an A on a history test or write a theme that will dazzle the English teacher, but because you belong to Him; He cares for you; He will not let you go.

Thomas Edison had a condition called dyslexia. He could barely read and write. He could not spell all the words in a five-word sentence correctly. Yet he was one of the great minds of modern times, responsible for hundreds of inventions. But what if he had gotten down on himself? What if he had decided he was "stupid" because he struggled with his work in school? What if he had given up on himself and never tried because he was convinced he was too dumb? He found his ability and used it as God would have had him use it—as best he could to accomplish what he was able to accomplish for the good of others.

The only person who is stupid is the one who believes that about himself or herself, gives up and doesn't care anymore—the one who believes the put-down artists and the people who can see things only one way. God has called you and equipped you for better things. To that end, seek His help to:

1. Look honestly at the things you don't do very well and accept yourself for what you are—for what God has made you. There is nothing to be gained by trying to be a person who is good at everything—except more frustration and more disappointment. All we are expected to do is the best we can with the abilities we have been given. Why should you apologize for what God has made you? You may wish He would have given you more of this or that ability or made it easier for you to excel at one thing or another. But He is proud of you. You can be too. You

owe no one an apology for what you are—only for what you do (don't do) with what you are.

2. Remember that a weakness is not a disability. It may be harder for you to memorize a list or solve a problem—but it won't be impossible. It may not seem fair that you have to study two hours and someone else needs to study only 10 minutes—but if that is the way it is, study the two hours, and do the best you can. One thing you can be sure of. The people who really excel—whether they are in the classroom, on the stage, or on the athletic field—do so because of hard work and dedication. No one is a star by accident. Your work may never make you a star, a scholar, or the best athlete—but it will make you the best whatever you can be. And that is what God wants for you.

3. Concentrate on your strengths. If you're good at cooking, building, listening, or writing, for example—put your energies into that skill, that ability. In its results you'll gain great satisfaction.

4. Never, ever say you are stupid. You'd have to be stupid to do that! We know that whatever you think you can't do, whatever your weaknesses or failures—being stupid is not one of them. To God, you're nothing less than a star. "Do everything without complaining . . . pure as God's perfect children, who live in a world of corrupt and sinful people. You must shine among them like stars lighting up the sky, as you offer them the message of life" (Phil. 2:14—16 TEV). Ever hear of a stupid star?

How do you know when to end a one-sided relationship?

 The easiest answer is: as soon as you get tired of being the one side who always gives and never gets anything in return. The truth is that this kind of a relationship can't last very long anyway. While it's true that in most relationships one person tends to be the giver and the other the taker, if one is all giver and another is all taker, it can't last.

Even in the best of relationships—those that last for years, even a lifetime—the giving and taking are probably not really equal. Watch couples or pairs of friends. One of them will tend to be the dominant person, the decision maker, the one who seeks attention and usually gets it. The other will be the giver—the one who is willing to step aside for the needs of the other, the one willing to pay attention, go along, and do it the other person's way.

And that's not all bad. It is practically impossible to set up a relationship that is exactly equal—in which every giving is matched by a giving in return, every taking by something taken. You'd have to keep score. Every time one person got his way, then the other person would have one coming. Not only would it get very confusing, it probably just wouldn't work. Some people like being the giver and wouldn't even understand that something was owed to them because they had given way or given attention out of love.

Some one-sidedness is probably inevitable in a relationship and probably healthy. But one-sidedness can also destroy the relationship. If the taking becomes taking advantage, taking for granted, taking without either recognition or response—then the relationship is finished.

That usually happens when two people "fall in love" and then one "falls out of it" again. At least that is the way we often describe what has happened.

Two people meet. They are interested in each other, get close to each other, "love" each other. At that point the love may be rather selfish and immature. It may be more infatuation than anything else.

"See, this girl is interested in me," the guy may be saying to himself. "I must be all right. She thinks she's in love with me."

And the girl may be thinking, "He cares about me. He must. He calls me all the time. He wants to do things with me. I must be doing something right."

The center of their concern is not the other person but themselves. They are not in love so much as in love with being loved. They enjoy the attention. They like being liked. They get satisfaction out of what the person who loves them can do for them.

But that kind of "relationship" cannot last. It is based on "what can I get out of this thing?" And getting (taking) can never be the foundation for any kind of lasting love.

Sometimes one of the people in that kind of a relationship really begins to care about the other. Perhaps the girl begins to focus not on what the guy can do for her but on him, his needs, his cares, and his hopes and dreams. She begins to move past infatuation to a real love for him and wants to do things for him, please him, and care for him. She feels great when she is with him—not just because others are envious or because she likes his attention but because she feels that she is a part of his life. She feels like a more complete person when she is around him and doing things for him. His faults tend to fade; his strengths become apparent. She really cares.

That's all to the good if it is happening to him too. If he is moving toward a more sincere love for her, then they are beginning to build a relationship that might last. But if he is still infatuated with himself, the relationship becomes lopsided (one-sided) and is doomed.

No matter how much in love she thinks she is, how sincere her care for him, or how dedicated she is to him—she cannot go on giving and getting nothing back, reaching out to him and seeing no response. She cannot keep on cherishing her love for him if he offers no love in return. Her love will turn to nagging demands, resentment when he doesn't respond, and finally to rejection. But her "love" won't die easily. We have a tendency to want to "save" a relationship, even one that has become one-sided. We think that if we give enough, offer enough, do enough, or love enough—somehow the other person will wake up and begin to love in return.

But it almost never happens. If he, for example, has become involved with her just for what it will do for his self-esteem and his place among his peers, there is nothing keeping him involved but self-interest—and self-interest will soon lead him to the next person who can make him feel even better about himself or more self-important. In the meantime he will use her, mistreat her, take her for granted, get what he can, and leave her.

She's better off to get out when she realizes that the relationship never was anything more than infatuation. And even though it hurts a lot, she'll want to build a relationship with someone else who will return her love.

But breaking up is another one of those things that is easier to say than to do. It can be particularly hard to give up on a relationship that used to be important; it's like admitting failure, like admitting that we've been rejected—that we could not make a success of even a simple relationship.

"Maybe there is something I could have done differently," we think to ourselves. "Maybe if I would have been nicer or more ready to give in, if I had been more responsive in the first place, or if I would have given more, maybe this wouldn't have happened. Maybe then he (she) would still be interested in me and not turn away from me. How can I face the others when I've blown this one? Won't they think I'm a reject if I have to admit that we're not going together anymore? Won't they think I'm a loser? Maybe the word will get out, and I'll never be able to date anyone again, much less get anyone to be really interested in me. Maybe this will finish off my social life for the rest of my life." And so the thoughts go. We feel guilty, like a failure, rejected, and disappointed all at the same time.

If the only help we had was to try to get hold of ourselves and try to make ourselves feel better, we'd be in a lot of trouble. It's hard to get over feeling guilty or feeling like a failure by just making up our minds to feel better. In fact, it's impossible. The more we try to get over it, the more we end up thinking about the whole thing and the worse we feel—until we're really in the pits. Then nothing at all seems to help.

The very best thing we can do when we've gotten to the end of our own trying, when we feel rejected by others and a failure, is to take it to God—not just to hear some words about how it will all be better "some day" or that He loves us anyway. We need to remind ourselves how much He cares about us—not just as one among the millions that He loves—but how much He cares about us as persons and how much He cares about the hurts that tear at us, the failures that drag us down, and the confusion that can make our lives miserable. He loves us and forgives us and keeps on forgiving us—because He loves us.

That kind of Good News can make a difference—even when we know we've blown it, when we wish things could be different, and when we'd like to have a chance to do things over or patch things up. When we know there is nothing we can do to make things right again, His care for us and His forgiveness can make a difference as we ask Him for the strength to throw that old, lop-sided, one-sided relationship out the window and move toward re-building our lives without that other person who used to be so important.

It won't happen overnight. We will not get over it just because we decide to, or even because we take it to God for His help. But things will change. Our life will get back together. We will find ourselves smiling again and looking forward again to the good things that will happen tomorrow and the day after that.

Best of all, we'll be free of the past and ready to look forward to a two-sided intertwining with another loved person in a lasting relationship.

Q *Why is there so much hurt in a boy-girl relationship? Why do two people have to hurt each other if they say they're in love?*

A Somehow we have gotten the idea that once people "fall in love" (whatever that means), they pass into the land of everlasting niceness where all is tender touches and loving looks. There they (in the words of the songs) "cherish" each other, "live for" each other, "can't do without" each other—you know how it goes.

Not only is that not true but the expectation itself that falling in love will automatically bring enjoyment, contentment, and bliss is setting people up for some very hard encounters with reality.

Actually, falling in love (if that means becoming attracted to and infatuated with someone) guarantees nothing. It will likely produce feelings both of ecstatic joy (he really does love me) and abject despair (why doesn't he call?). But there is certainly nothing built into the process that is lasting, dependable, or even predictable. About the only thing you can be sure of when you fall in love is that you are going to have to live through some confusion and some hurt either before that new love grows to a more mature love or before it dies away.

All the sloppy songs aside, falling in love is only the very first step in building a lasting relationship with another person. It is only the start (and usually a bumpy one at that) of a long journey to the mutual care and concern that characterizes real, lasting love.

"Falling in love" (infatuation, "love at first sight") is really nothing more than attraction to someone and interest in that person. It feels good largely because it is new. It's exciting because it fires up a lot of emotions that have been quiet for a long time and starts a lot of sexual feelings perking. In all, at least at first, it is really great to be the center of someone else's attention—and to have someone so "wonderful" at the center of our lives.

But there's not much substance to that stage of loving someone. There's a lot of "taking one's emotional pulse" going on. "How do I feel now? Don't I feel wonderful when she looks at

47

me? Why do I feel so bad?" and a lot of worry about whether he will stay interested or whether she will change.

We lose our appetites because we feel so good or so bad; we daydream because we think we want to be somewhere else; we let things slide because that other person seems to become the most important thing in our life. It's all part of falling in love.

But love at the "falling in love stage" is a lot like a car without brakes going down a steep hill. That love might stay "on the road" for a while—but something has to give. First love might hang in there for a while, but it just can't stay "on the right track." There is too much feeling involved, too much selfishness, and too much recklessness! Lasting love, in contrast to the heady swirl of "falling in love," is built on commitment, real caring, trust, and respect.

So first love must either grow or crash. And, interestingly, either way—it's going to hurt.

Certainly, there is nothing pleasant about love (even first love) that fades and dies. It hurts to see a person we cared about drift away. It's pretty hard to take when we feel rejected by a person who was once so central in our lives. And even though there isn't much more than focused self-interest in new love—it hurts when it dies, and it can make us turn (at least temporarily) sour on ourselves and life, push us into the pits, and generally make things look bleak and dismal for a time.

But as painful as it is to see love die, it is almost as painful to live through it as it grows. Love grows only as it is tested, and testing hurts—at least a little.

The myth says that the center of lasting love is the feeling of attachment and identification we have for another person when we fall in love. Not so. The most important aspects of love that lasts are mutual respect, trust, honest communication, and acceptance. None of them happen automatically. Any of these aspects are going to tax our patience and our perseverance as they develop in relationship with another person.

Infatuation says, "This is the greatest, best, and most loving person in the world." Acceptance says, "This person is not always the best and not always as attentive and concerned as I'd like. He (she) is sometimes rude, sometimes careless, and sometimes infuri-

atingly slow to respond to me. *But* I love him (her) anyway."
Such acceptance is not automatic, nor is it brought on by good
intentions. It is the result of living through the faults of another
person (faults that often hurt) and learning to love in spite of those
faults.

Similarly, infatuation sees the other person as responsible,
loving, and trustworthy—though it has no reason to do so except
that the person is so "wonderful." And it is only through experience that the real trust that a lasting relationship needs is built.
Trust is mutual—it is returned confidence for confidence shown. It
is learned by trusting and being trusted in return. And sometimes
the giving and receiving of trust can be painful.

So it is also with mutual respect. Infatuation tends to put the
other person on a pedestal. Obviously, one so wonderful ought to
be head and shoulders above everyone else. But illusions about
the greatness of another are not respect. Respect comes when we
know another person well enough to look past his faults to see his
strengths and love him for them. Respect sees the person honestly
and cherishes him.

Sometimes people want to know if they are really "in love."
They want to know if the feeling they have for another person is
the real thing. It's hard to say. Love that lasts is not exactly the
same for every person. But here are some good questions to ask
yourself when the matter comes to mind: Do I know this person?
Really know her? Do I know what she's like when she's angry,
when she makes a mistake, when she shows her weaknesses? Do
I know her well enough to dislike her—and still love her? If the
answer is yes, the love is pretty solid.

Part of the pain of a boy-girl relationship comes from the selfishness of the early "falling in love." It comes from the immaturity
of the love, the demands that kind of love can make, and the in-
ability of that kind of love to put the other person first, to understand the other's feelings, and to be sensitive to the other's needs.

But a part of the hurt of boy-girl relationships is the growing
that love must do before it can be the kind of love on which to
build a life.

Lasting love is a great deal like God's love for us. It is a giving love (even giving to the point of pain) because that other per-

son is so specially loved—not because he is so great, wonderful, or perfect—but because we know him well, have been through a lot together, and love him anyway.

Interestingly, even then, the hurt does not completely disappear from a relationship. In this life it never will. Even people who cherish each other, loving each other in a lasting and special way, hurt each other. They make mistakes, take each other for granted sometimes, forget to respond, turn away. As long as we live in a sinful world, we will find ourselves doing things we don't really mean and don't really want to do.

That brings us to the most important aspect of lasting love. It forgives. The treasure that God gives us in Christ is not only a promise of heaven some day or the special calling to be His witnesses. A special treasure He gives is His forgiveness—not only the forgiveness that Christ gained for us and by which He sets aside our failures but also the forgiveness He gives us to share with each other.

How else can we sustain a love over all those years? If the hurts cannot be done away with, if the pains of the past must be carried, and if the mistakes and failures tend to become barriers between us—how can love survive?

We can look straight at the failure of our loved one (as God does at ours) and set that aside—put it away (even though it hurts) and start over again, not because we are perfect or able to do wonders on our own, but because we have been forgiven by God in Jesus Christ.

The hurts in a relationship will not go away—at least not in this life. But they can be done away with by the power we have been given—the power of the Spirit that lets us forgive (and forget) the wrongs of the past and begin each day to build a new life together. That life together may produce its hurts—but, more important, it will produce the joy of belonging, the pleasure of mutual caring, and the treasure of shared love that lasts not just for now, but for eternity with Him.

Q *Will anyone ever fall in love with me?*

A I can hear a lot of hurt in that question. I remember how it felt when it was my question, especially when I had messed up, or when someone had made fun of me, or when a girl had turned me down. Then, like a nagging voice, I'd hear it clearly: "Will anyone ever love me?" Or more like: "Will anyone I love (would like to love) ever find me lovable enough (worth enough, good enough, valuable enough, good-looking enough, etc.) to love me?"

The answer the people out there who cared about me used to give me was yes. "Everyone falls in love sometime," they would say. "There's someone in the world for everyone," they would tell me. "Don't worry about it. You'll find that Miss Right." And maybe they were right. Maybe it is easy to fall in love if you find that other person who is looking too. Maybe in spite of—or because of—the feeling that no one can love either one of us, we will cling to one another. But are two lonely people, clinging together because they want to chase away pain, being loved? Is that the only kind of love I can find? Can I really be loved, for myself, as a person? Can someone love *me*?

A young woman came for counseling. She was very troubled, she said. She needed someone to help her. To look at her, one would suppose she didn't have a care in the world. She was attractive, well-dressed, had a good job with an airline, and had her own apartment—everything a young person could have wanted.

"I'm seriously thinking about killing myself," she said. "If I weren't so afraid of dying, I'd do it."

She found her life pure misery. She could not find anyone with whom to form a lasting relationship. She felt guilty about the boyfriends who passed like a careless parade through her life. In spite of her looks, intelligence, and other advantages, she thought herself worthless—unlovable.

Obviously, she was focusing on the wrong things. She saw her whole life—even her "advantages"—through a haze of guilt and self-pity that made her hate herself and draw back from rela-

51

tionships with others because she thought herself unlovable—and ended up unloved.

The first step in finding someone to love you is not looking around for Mr. or Miss Right. It is loving yourself. Easy to say—hard to do.

Fortunately, especially in this, God has not left us on our own. If the Gospel says something important for this world and if the death and resurrection of Jesus Christ for us have an effect on our life now, it is exactly this: God declares us worthwhile and lovable. It doesn't matter how "good" we are according to the standard of the world; it doesn't matter if we are the best athletes—or the best anything; and it doesn't matter if we are beautiful or ugly, pleasant or unpleasant to look at, popular or not. He loves each of us in Jesus Christ so much that He literally went to the cross for us—that makes us both lovable and worthwhile.

If God—who knows both us and the hurtful and foolish things we have done, who knows our secret thoughts and our secret sins, and who knows us even down to our skin and beyond—loves us, then we can love ourselves, and we are "good" enough to be loved by another. Believing that means:

1. Returning often to God's Word. Indeed it tells us something about ancient deeds, ancient people, and distant happenings. But, more important, it tells us again and again that God loves—He loved the stumbling Moses, the faltering Jeremiah, the suicidal Elijah, and the denying Peter. And He loves us—regardless of how we feel about ourselves on a given day. Even when we are in the pits, He loves us and will not let go of us.

2. Paying attention to the "good stuff" about ourselves. All of us have things we'd like to hide from others—anything from a too-big nose to a high-pitched voice. We may feel we are too tall, too short, too shy, too loud, too soft, too unfriendly—whatever. But as long as we concentrate on our weaknesses and failings, we will be cutting ourselves off from others and make ourselves unlovable.

We seek God's help to look at the strengths we have, the good about ourselves, and all the other stuff that makes us feel worthwhile. As we look at our strengths and look past our weaknesses, the voice in us that used to say, "You're no good, you're worthless, stupid," begins to say, "See, you're not so bad. You may not have the rock stars worried about the competition—but, kid, let me tell you, you're doing all right."

Q *Does God really care about me?*

A Most adults will probably give you a quick yes to that question. It's pretty easy to answer that way—easy to repeat the Sunday-school lines: "Jesus loves me, this I know, For the Bible tells me so." But, of course, you've heard all that before.

Maybe your question sounds more like: "How can God care about me, especially when I feel so unlovable?" That question certainly comes from uncertain feelings you have about yourself—but it also reflects an increasingly common and decidedly unhelpful picture of God. For whatever reason, many people today are trying to convince themselves that God is really just a nice old guy in the clouds, who watches us with a distant and somewhat disinterested eye. He pats us on the head when we have a problem or two and gives us good things when He happens to think of it. In all, this kind "Santa" likes us, thinks we're doing the best we can, doesn't really expect too much as long as we try to do good, and will ultimately make things work out all right.

For people busy with their own lives, caught up in their own doing—when they're "doing their own thing" as the saying goes—that kind of a God is just fine. He watches but doesn't interfere. He gives but expects almost nothing in return. He has a plan for us but doesn't push it very hard. He doesn't get too excited about anything we do. He's like an absentee parent who sends his regular support or calls us occasionally to see how we're doing, but usually minds his own business. Best of all, like the good guy He is, He excuses us for our little indiscretions and errors. "After all," He might say, "you're trying. What's a little mistake now and then? Just hang in there, and everything will be fine."

But sometimes things are not fine. Sometimes the little indiscretions of life get bigger; the mistakes are not errors—they are great, gigantic foul-ups. Sometimes we don't just stray—we run crashing off into stupidity. We blow it. We really mess up. Then what?

What good is a God who pats us on the head then? What good does it do to have a Santa in the sky if we've wiped ourselves out?

We're devastated. We don't know how we're going to put the pieces back together again. And there's "Santa" saying, "Well, it doesn't really matter. Just do your best, and it will all work out." If that's all God can do, then He is as mythical as Santa and just as useless. Worse, if God's response to our failures is a bemused excusing, then He really doesn't care.

People like to think that excusing and forgiving are the same. They are not. When we bump someone, we might say, "Forgive me!" We mean, "Please overlook my error; it was inadvertent." We are really saying, "Excuse me," not "Forgive me." Forgiving is not excusing. Forgiving hurts. Forgiving comes from down inside where we're torn apart by what another person has done—and sets that hurt right again.

When you've been betrayed (again) by a friend, when that friend promised "never ever to tell anyone" and told anyway, when you trusted that friend and she failed you—disappointed you and destroyed your reputation—and when she then comes and says: "Forgive me," that's when you know the difference between excusing and forgiving. You would never be able to excuse something like that. How could you say, "It's all right. It doesn't matter"?

Of course, it matters. It matters a great deal. Forgiveness sets aside the hurt in spite of the fact that it matters so much that it almost turns you inside out to reach out to that person again—to call her friend again.

God forgives. He does not excuse. God loves us, but He does not necessarily approve of everything we do. He does not act like Santa in the sky, patting us on the head when we do our best. Our best is simply not good enough—we muddle it, mess things up, and fail ourselves, others, and God.

God does not "like" our failure. In fact, He hates it. God despises our sinfulness and the result of our sin. No kidding around. That sin hurts Him the same way that the betrayal of a friend hurts us. And He most definitely does not say, "Well, it doesn't matter." It does matter. It matters to Him. Fortunately, we matter more.

That's just it. God doesn't merely like us, tolerate us, put up with us, watch us, and prod us to do the best we can. He loves us, and He calls us to be what He expects us to be—perfect. We are the ones who are called to live in perfect harmony with His will and in perfect service to others.

Of course, we fail. We are still pushed around by sin in us, but the miracle is that God does not pat us, prod us, or overlook us. He looks squarely at the failure, sees Jesus, and forgives us.

Surely His love hurts Him. His love is so great that He has obligated Himself to forgive us because of the death and resurrection of Jesus. Only that sacrifice measures the depth of His love for us.

How can God love you when you've really messed up (again)? How can He stick with you when you've let everyone down, made a fool of yourself, and hurt those you love the most? How can He love you when you're ready to give up on yourself? How can He care when you don't care anymore?

How? He can because He loves with the depth of the love of Jesus, who went to the cross for you. He forgives in spite of the pain of your failure. He loves with an everlasting love, a love that will not give up on you—even when you are tempted to give up on yourself.

Does God care? God does more than care. He loves and, what is more, He forgives. He can do nothing less because of Jesus.

Another way that the "Does God really care about me?" question can sound is this: "God is so great. He is God of the universe, God of the stars and the heavens and the history of the world. How can that great God care about little, unimportant, and unimpressive me?"

The psalmist put it this way: "When I look at Thy heavens, the work of Thy fingers, the moon and the stars which Thou hast established; what is man that Thou art mindful of him, and the son of man that Thou dost care for him?" (Ps. 8:3-4).

Humankind has struggled with that question since the beginning. And it has been answered in many ways. Some see God as a distant presence that can only be reached by "getting out of self"—by somehow first escaping the physical trappings of being human and then being joined to God. Others see the great gulf between insignificant humankind and the great holy God as a challenge that must be overcome by dedication and hard work. They feel that if they are good enough or loving enough or righteous enough, they will come so close to God that He will love them and take care of them or give them whatever it is they need.

In countless ways the religions of humankind try to "get us up there" somehow with the perfect God by right living or right thinking. Unfortunately, all fail in the same way—because none seems to be able to determine just how good one must be and how righteous or how much right thinking one must achieve in order to make it. So the question "How can God care about unimportant, imperfect me?" is never answered. The religions of humankind really don't know.

The Bible has a different answer: it tells us that there is nothing within us, nothing we can do, no amount of right thinking on our part that can make God care for us. Left to ourselves, we are full of sin, separated from God, distant from His presence, and anything but perfect. We are not even getting better—as some would have us believe. Of ourselves we are cut off from God and have no way to make that separation any less.

The miracle of God's love is that He comes to us, rather than the other way around. One of the treasured names of Jesus in the Old Testament is Emmanuel ("God with us"). That's not just a cute name we recall at Christmastime. It is a description of God's answer to the "How can God care for us?" question.

He *does* care for us. It is His nature to love so much that He not only looks at us, not only loves us, but He rescues us while we are helpless. "While we are yet sinners," St. Paul says, "Christ died for us." That perfect love is great beyond belief and comforting beyond anything that we could create out of our own wishes or imagination.

If we, indeed, were trying to be good enough for God to love us, great enough for Him to care about us, and righteous enough for Him to be present with us—when would we make it? When would we arrive? Our inner self tells us we'd never make it. In all honesty, we realize that we aren't even able to keep our promises to ourselves, let alone any long-term commitments to God.

His love for us is perfect because it reaches us in spite of the fact that we are neither great enough nor good enough for Him even to care. He loves us so perfectly that He gives His very life for us.

Does He care? Yes, in fact He does even more than care about us. He offers Himself for us, comes to us personally in Baptism, and sustains us by the power of His Word and Sacrament.

A Note on "Why" Questions

Most of the questions in this book start with the word *why*. Basically there is nothing wrong with a "why" question. Asking a child why he or she threw the baseball through the window can give you some helpful information. Even a "why" question directed to a formerly close but now distant girlfriend or boyfriend can be the start of an interesting conversation.

But all of the "why" questions here are really directed to God; therefore, these "why" questions deserve some special attention.

Some God-directed "why" questions are probably not really very important. They're more like curiosity or idle musing. They're the kind of questions that come to you when you don't have anything better to do: Why did God make the world in the first place? Why did He make space so big? Why didn't He just give up after Adam and Eve fell into sin?

Questions like that are pretty tough to answer. Virtually all the information we have about God we find in the Scriptures. The Bible just doesn't deal with such questions. Questions that pretend that we can somehow get into the mind of God and understand both His plans and purposes are off track from the outset.

One thing we know for sure: much of what God thinks, plans, and does is far beyond us. We cannot get our minds around Him nor make Him obey our thought processes. Answers to such questions are speculation at best—and probably largely a waste of time.

Other God-directed "why" questions are more important—certainly, more important to the questioner. They are the kinds of questions that come out of hurt or disappointment or grief. They sound like this: Why wasn't I made more beautiful (attractive, good-looking, etc.)? Why did this terrible thing have to happen to me? Why can't the things I want ever come true for me?

Certainly, those are all good questions. They cry out for an answer. But they all want to have God explain Himself or at least explain why certain things have happened in our lives.

"Why" questions like that make some assumptions that may

not be true. For example, a question like, "Why did this happen to me?" assumes that God is somehow responsible for that hurtful or hateful event. Though it is true that God is in ultimate control, He certainly is not pushing buttons that bring on all the devastation, death, and evil that happen in the world.

God knows what happens. In a sense He permits it—to the extent that He does not interfere with storms, earthquakes, auto accidents, even illnesses. He is aware of what is happening. He occasionally intervenes to cause a miraculous rescue or to bring about a miraculous cure. But God does not cause evil to happen. Evil happens because the world is sinful—full of sin since Adam's time.

Paul says, "We are not fighting against human beings but against the wicked spiritual forces in the heavenly world, the rulers, authorities, and cosmic powers of this dark age" (Eph. 6:12 TEV). Peter presents a similar warning: "The devil prowls around like a roaring lion, seeking some one to devour" (1 Peter 5:8). We must arm ourselves, Paul says, with "helmets" and "breastplates" for the battle we will be involved in all of our lives (cf. Eph. 6:13—17).

And this is no mock battle. We are caught up in a fight to the death—not with God, but with sin, evil, and the powers of Satan. And one thing is sure. We will be hurt, wounded, even killed in the battle. Being a Christian is no escape clause from the world—no way of getting out of the problems and difficulties, the death and destruction that come to all people.

Evil is powerful. It does its deed. People die; devastation happens; illness comes to all of us; and no one will get out of this life alive. That's the truth. And there is nothing we can do to change that truth . . . except cling to God's love in Jesus Christ, which assures us that no matter what happens in this life, we cannot be separated from His love and His eternal salvation. That's what Rom. 8:38—39 tells us.

So the basic problem in asking God why you are ill, why your father died, or why you are having this problem or that trouble is that when we do that we are holding Him responsible for things He has not caused to happen.

God is on your side. He loves you in Jesus. When Jesus was

on earth, He spent His time making right what sin had undone, broken, devastated, and destroyed. He healed; He made people alive; He rescued; He made people whole. That is God's will for us—a will that will be fulfilled completely in heaven.

In the meantime, things will not always be the way we want them. God may not interfere in the workings of this evil world and make miracles for us when we want Him to. We may not be able to escape the pain, tears, hurts, and problems of life.

But this we know for sure:

1. He will not let us be destroyed, overcome by the evil of the world. He promised that (1 Cor. 10:13), and He keeps His word.
2. He understands and stands with us in our temptation, hurt, and despair. Heb. 4:15 tells us that—and tells us the truth.
3. Though He doesn't cause the evil in our life, sometimes He uses it to strengthen us—refine us. We are promised we will be stronger for coming through the hardships of life. We are tested as in a refiner's fire (cf. Mal. 3:2–3). And everything that happens, even that difficult time of testing, will work to our good (Rom. 8:28).
4. We will finally win because Jesus has won. "Thanks be to God, who gives us the victory through Jesus Christ our Lord" (1 Cor. 15:57).

With those assurances we can go on when life seems to strike us down, when we don't get what we think we need, when death takes a loved, and when our plans and dreams don't work out. Even when we are ill, sick unto death, we can have confidence that God holds us tight and will never let us go.

Why do bad things happen to us? Because of evil, sin, and Satan. That's why!

Why, when we hurt, does God not interfere, not give us what we want, not change things for our benefit? We don't have complete answers, but we trust, relying on God's love, cherishing His presence, and depending on His promises. With Him we face the mystery of the "whys" of life.

Q *Why did my father die?*

A I don't know the answer to that question. My father also died young. He was just getting to be my friend. We were just getting to the place where we could enjoy one another's company, where we could do some of the things we'd always planned, where he could see some of what he'd worked for all his life really start to happen.

But at 54 he died. And I wanted to know why.

Why my father? Why him? He was loved so much, needed so much. Thousands of other fathers out there don't even matter. No one even cares about them. Why?

Why now, when he was still so young? Why now, while I still needed him so much? Why?

It's pretty easy to let that kind of why question start to eat at you. Someone must be responsible. Someone must have caused this hurt. Didn't God know how much we needed him? Didn't God care?

Maybe God doesn't care. Maybe He's angry with me, out to get back at me for something I've done.

But I haven't done anything that bad, have I? It just isn't fair. How can He do this to me?

The why questions turn to angry questions, and God seems very far away.

That kind of thinking gets us quickly into the pits. There in the darkness of our own self-pity, God seems to say, "I couldn't care less." We feel all alone and abandoned. Not even other people seem to be able to get through to us.

The trip out of the pits is not easy. It takes time, tears, patience, and a lot of love from a lot of people to get us out of the hole of hurt we are in. All the preaching and teaching and speaking and telling doesn't seem to do any good.

Only when the light starts to come again do we begin to accept what has happened and to understand that we have not walked off into the darkness away from the light of God's love and that we have not fallen out of His hand, which continues to hold us.

It is terribly painful when someone near us dies. It is like having a part of ourselves torn away. It is like staring into an emptiness in ourselves that will never be filled—except, perhaps, with our own tears.

Death is like that. It is a robber. It takes from us the people we hold most dear. It rips our life apart and brings us to our knees in grief, anger, and despair. It is a destroyer. We cannot even understand it, much less overcome it.

All we can do is cling to the faith we have that Jesus did defeat even death. That's what the cross is about. Certainly, Jesus' death is not just a story about how some important person died. He did not just go to the cross to give us an example of how we should die when the time comes. There on the cross the greatest battle in the world was going on. There the King and Creator of life was dying *for us*—not only for our benefit, but in our place, as our substitute—so that we might live forever.

This boggles the minds of those who have no hope, who stare at the specter of death and see only defeat, and who look into the future beyond death and see only blackness and emptiness. We confuse them when we come through the death of a loved one with a word of rejoicing.

Oh, sure, we're sad. We cry real tears. We suffer real pain. We cling to each other and weep with one another.

But we rejoice too. We sing songs of victory, pray prayers of thanksgiving, and remember times of joy—because we have not lost.

In spite of all evidence to the contrary, because of the resurrection of Jesus Christ, we trust that we have not lost. Even in death we are the victors—the winners, the ones who finally come out on top, for not even death can separate us from the love of God in Christ Jesus (Rom. 8:39).

So cry. Shed your tears. Remember your father. Remember the good times you had with him. Share the love you shared with him. Cling to another person, and weep over the loss of him.

Then look to Jesus.

Q *Why is my skin a color I don't want it to be?*

 A Little Mike, five years old, thought that all his problems were caused by his new, red baseball jacket. He felt that way because, whenever his mother would dress him to go outside and play with his friend, she'd put on him his nice, new baseball jacket. And out he'd march—and run into trouble. He'd get into a fight with the kid next door, or someone would take his bike, or someone would call him a name. Now that sort of thing never happened at home. No one at home called him names or fought with him—so he concluded that the source of all his problems was his jacket. He had a problem all right—but it had nothing to do with his jacket.

I don't mean to minimize the trouble you might have with the color of your skin. Unless one has experienced it, it's difficult to understand what it's like to be hated, scorned, rejected, even physically hurt because our skin is a certain color. One thing we can be rather sure about: in ignorance, people do some very stupid and very damaging things, and skin color isn't the only thing that brings out the worst in them.

For instance, people who are too short are teased, hurt, and rejected because of their size. Fat people are outcast because of their bulk. Tall people stick out like a sore thumb, as the saying goes. And then there are those with noses too big, feet too big, hands too small, and those with freckles, big ears—whatever. Everyone has something about them that they would make over if they had a chance. No one is perfect.

True, fat people are sometimes teased, sometimes rejected, because they are fat—and short people because they are short and black people because they are black. But the real problem has as little to do with fatness, shortness, and skin color as the boy's problem had to do with the jacket.

Some fat people couldn't care less what people think and say. Some short people are perfectly happy being short. And some black people are completely satisfied with their black skin.

Of course, it's not easy to be black- (or yellow- or brown-)

skinned in a world where white-skinned people get all the breaks. Neither is it easy to be fat in a skinny world or short in a tall world. But all of us have two choices as we look at the part of ourselves that we'd like to make different—we can fight against it (suffer with it and let it ruin our lives), or we can make the best of it and in the process make the best of ourselves.

Making the best of it means:

1. Seeking God's help to accept ourselves as we are—black skin, big nose, fat legs, big ears, and all. God made us. He may not have done it perfectly according to our way of thinking, but He did make us, and that surely ought to be good enough for us.

2. Seeking His help to look past the things about ourselves that we don't like to the things we do like. Maybe we will never like the color of our skin or the color of our hair or the size of our eyes—but we should be thankful for the talents and abilities He has given us, and we can be proud of ourselves, not in a selfish "I'm better than you" way, but in a way that is thankful for what we are and can do. And we can make the best of our God-given gifts.

It may seem to you that no one really knows what it's like to have the hurt you have to carry. It may seem to you that others have all the advantages because they have the right color skin—or whatever else they have that is right and good. But looking at yourself and others that way will only lead to more and more bitterness and unhappiness.

The little guy with the jacket went outside without it. He still had problems—in himself. When he learned to be sensitive to the needs of others, to stop grabbing things for himself, and to reach out to other people in love—the problems stopped for him, and he began to enjoy being around others.

That's the key. Seek God's help to love yourself enough to reach out to others in spite of whatever it is you don't like about yourself. Care about others, be sensitive to them, and be a friend to them the way you'd like them to be a friend to you.

All of a sudden you'll find that the others are trying to reach out to you past the hurt and disappointment they have in themselves. And they will love you, with or without your new jacket.

Q *Why isn't life/death fair?*
Why is life taken from really good people?
Why did the baby that was so wanted die?

A It seems like life ought to be, at least, fair. It seems like with all the trouble most people have, all the heartache and hardship, God ought to make an effort to deal fairly with everyone. Good people ought to get blessed—they ought to get something for all their effort to be good. Innocent people should not suffer. They don't deserve to suffer. Doesn't even trying to do the right thing get you anything? Doesn't God care enough to make life fair?

God does care. But life is not always fair—not because God doesn't want it to be, but because of sin.

Sin separates and destroys. It causes evil to happen in our lives, in the world, in relationships, in everything. People get hurt because of sin. Sometimes the wrong people get hurt. People die because of sin. Sometimes the wrong people die.

Some people would like to believe that God is kind of a scorekeeper. They'd like to think that He keeps accounts somewhere and that, as you do good, you earn credit toward blessings and miracles and toward getting the things you want. As you do bad, you earn "demerits" that can lead to trouble, sickness, and punishment. Of course, if that were true, it would make life both very manageable and very scary. You could certainly work hard to do right in order to please God. But how would you know when you had enough credits? How would you avoid the demerits, the troubles, and the punishment? How could you ever be sure you had the right balance so that you could get out of life what you need?

The real problem is that people begin to believe that they *have* earned credits with their goodness. They believe that they *have* said enough prayers, attended enough worship services, or helped enough needy people to have "gotten in good" with God.

Then something terrible happens. Without warning they become ill, lose a loved one, or get into some other trouble. "What

68

did I do to deserve this?" they say. "How could God treat me like this when I've done so much good?"

And if God were a scorekeeper, the question would make some sense. But God does not keep score. And, finally, it's a good thing He doesn't.

According to His records there's nothing to keep score about. "All have sinned . . . " (Rom. 3:23). "If we say we have no sin, we deceive ourselves . . . " (1 John 1:8). And sin is deadly stuff. It always has its effect. If God is waiting until we accumulate enough good to overcome the sin and the evil in us, He will wait forever.

Even though it seems hard to accept, no one "deserves" blessings from God. No one has done enough good. No one has it made.

We have trouble with that. We see people as different. Some seem better than others, some more loving than others, and some more deserving than others. And according to our laws that is true. Some are more righteous, nicer, and more helpful. And that is good. But God looks at us through His demand that we be "perfect." And none of us is perfect.

His demand seems unrealistic. It seems cruel for God to expect us to be perfect. He knows we are not perfect, and He wants us to know that on our own we cannot be perfect.

That is God's way of doing things. If He waited for us, we'd never make it. But He does not wait. Because He knew we could not be perfect on our own, He makes us perfect by grace through faith in Jesus Christ, who lived a perfect life, suffered, and died in our place as our Savior and rose triumphant from the grave.

Now when God looks at us, He does not see the mistakes, the confusion, the weakness, the sins, and the failure in us. He sees Jesus Christ, and we are perfect—made perfect every day by His forgiveness—and are promised life that cannot be taken away from us.

We still live in a sinful world. We are not yet free of the part of ourselves that would run from God, seek our own way, and take things for ourselves. We are not yet free from the sin that would destroy us, and that sin causes things to happen that don't seem fair to us. The wrong people still die. The good don't seem to get what they deserve. The right people don't seem to get the rewards.

But at God's hand we are not given what we deserve but what Jesus deserves—not what we think God should be offering us but what Jesus has claimed for us. Nothing can take away those blessings—neither sickness nor death nor any power or tragedy. Nothing can separate us from God's love in Christ Jesus, our Lord (Rom. 8:38—39).

That's the good news we cling to when life seems unfair. That's the hope we have when things don't work out the way we want them to, when the wrong people seem to suffer, and when apparently undeserved trouble happens. We cling to His eternal and unchangeable love—a love that reached us while we were sinners (Rom. 5:8) and will never let us go.

Q *Is it OK for a Christian to love a non-Christian—even an atheist?*

A In a certain sense we're supposed to "love" everyone. Scripture tells us to love one another as God has loved us. In the same way that God loves all people—cares about them enough to send His Son for them (even though He does not always "like" what they do)—we are to love others.

But that's really not what the question means. Rather you are asking: "Is it all right to 'fall in love' with someone who is not a Christian—to love him or her in the special way, in a way that would cause you to make a commitment to him or her?"

It's pretty hard to decide with whom you're going to fall in love. Love—the sense of oneness that we experience with that one special person—doesn't always happen because it's either supposed to or not supposed to. Lots of people have looked for Mr. or Miss Right—have chosen just the kind of person they would like to fall in love with. They have found a person with the right kind of background, someone with compatible values, similar faith, and similar family background. They have searched out the kind of person with whom they can share interests and activities—who seems to really "fit." And—nothing happens. They just don't "fall for" that person.

Susan had an experience like that. She was a bright young woman who always seemed to have things under control. She graduated from high school, got a job, and seemed to be moving ahead with her life as planned. She decided she was going to marry Larry. He was just the right kind of a guy; he was the same age, had the same interests, even went to the same church. Larry worked in a clothing store, but he attended college at night, studying pre-law. He had the "right stuff," as they say. He was the kind of a guy any girl would like to marry—until Susan met Mike. Mike had nothing going for him—at least as far as Susan was concerned. Mike was a high-school dropout. He rode motorcycles and had dirty fingernails. He called her Sue and half the time forgot to call her at all. But in spite of herself, she fell for Mike, and Larry was left out in the cold.

71

A lot of love—at least early love—is emotion, and emotion does not happen according to plan. Many people fall in love and still are unable to have a workable relationship with the one they love. "I love this woman," said one young man who came for counseling. "I just can't stand to live with her." He had a point. We may be attracted to a person who has some of our own personality characteristics, yet find it hard to tolerate those characteristics over a long period of time.

Someone once oversimplified relationships by saying that people are basically either *trees* or *vines*—they either stand alone or like to cling to someone, or lean on someone. It was his opinion that in a relationship it didn't matter who was the tree and who was the vine—but you needed both to make a marriage work. If you had either two trees or two vines, you were headed for disaster.

Well, there's an element of truth in this little analogy. If you look carefully at a relationship that lasts, you will likely find that one person is the stand-up-and-make-decisions person in the relationship and the other is the leaner. Of course, this is not always true, and these roles sometimes reverse in time and in given situations, but there is at least a surface truth here.

In any case, falling in love with the wrong "kind" of person may entail more than his religious beliefs. The wrongness of the other may have to do with his personality, his expectations of a marriage, his attitudes toward others, his willingness to make decisions, or a hundred other things. For that reason, it is worthwhile to know about as many of those "differences" as possible *before* marriage. It prevents many unpleasant surprises later.

In most cases it is easiest to establish a long-term love relationship with someone who is quite like ourselves—someone with the same ideas, attitudes, values, expectations, hopes, and dreams. That similarity of background and world view makes for the kind of solidarity that will hold a relationship together when the "glow" of first love has faded.

After the "honeymoon is over," as they say—after the "romance" has cooled a bit, after each of you has fallen off the pedestal you started out on, after you have taken a good look at each other's failings, faults, and foolishness—it is your ability to simply enjoy one another's company, to look forward to things together, to do things together, and to be "friends" with each other that will sustain the relationship.

That's why falling in love with an atheist can be the first step toward real trouble. You might really feel you love that person, in spite of his lack of religious beliefs. You might feel that your love will sustain you no matter what comes in the future, that he is such a good person that it doesn't matter what he believes, and that you can overlook any fault he might have because you love him so much.

That might even be true, at least for a while. But the love that floated you to the altar, that makes everything around the person you love seem to take on a kind of rosy glow, and that makes all problems seem to disappear won't last. When he forgets to take out the garbage for the umpteenth time, comes home without what you asked him to pick up, throws his clothes around again, and seems to be in the bathroom every time you want to get in there—love becomes something much more realistic and much more practical than it was at first.

Then the problem of his religious beliefs might get to be a real difficulty, especially if he is aggressive and argumentative about his views. Suppose he begins to make fun of your faith, to prevent you from introducing your children to God's Word and will for them, and to interfere with your own faith life? What then?

No one can keep you from falling in love with someone who is not a believer. Other than avoiding being around people like that, you probably can't either. But you can make some intelligent decisions about such "love" before it gets to the place where it pulls you into problems that may affect your whole life.

It's pretty hard to break off with a person you're in love with. It's pretty hard to say good-bye to someone who has become so special, who means so much, and who cares so much in return. But sometimes it is the only thing you can do. If you take a good look at the relationship and determine that, for whatever reason, it just can't survive, then it is better to end it as soon as possible—before it is almost impossible to end. Better kiss him good-bye now—than suffer the consequences of your failure to do so for the rest of your life.

So enjoy it when you fall in love. Make the most of the romance that comes your way. Revel in the attention and the caring that you receive from someone who has fallen in love with you. But some time—some important time before you find yourself saying "I do"—think carefully about what your love, your relationship, and your life together will be like in 5 or 10 years—or more.

If that picture is unclear, if there are problems you can't see your way out of, or if you see dangers that you may not be able to deal with—then it might be best to let that love gently fade into a fine memory and to do a little more looking for Mr. or Miss Right.

Q *Why do teachers always insist they're right?*

A I suppose the same question could be asked about pastors, policemen, even parents. People in authority—especially people who are supposed to be in charge-are reluctant to admit it when they are wrong.

Well, think of this another way for a minute. Suppose you had a teacher who was always wrong. Every time a question came up, the teacher would give the wrong answer. How long would you or anyone in the class listen to him? How long would you believe what he had to say about anything? Obviously, he would quickly become useless as a teacher because what he said was not dependable.

Think of it from the teacher's point of view. If you were in a classroom, charged with teaching some more or less interested kids something, would you want to take the chance that they might decide that you were either ignorant or uninformed? Would you want to take a chance that they might think they know more about the subject you are supposed to be teaching than you do?

How would it sound to the parents of those kids if they went home and said, "Well, we put it over on old——today. He's such a blutz. We know more about what's going on in class than he does." How long do you think you'd last as a teacher at that school?

It takes a rather self-confident teacher to admit when he's wrong. It takes a teacher who knows he is both informed and prepared to be able to stand up in front of the class and admit he's made a mistake. He must be willing to take the chance that the class will understand that the mistake is not a habit, that the failing is not an indicator of his ability, and that in most things, in spite of the failure, he will be able to give the students not only the knowledge they need to pass the course but also what they will need to know about the subject in the future.

You might help teachers be a little more honest about what

75

they know and don't know if you ask your questions and make your challenges in a helpful instead of an accusing way. Few teachers will be able to deal with a student whose comment sounds like: "See! We caught you in another mistake. How could you say something like that?"

Most teachers will respond well to a student who genuinely disagrees or has difficulty understanding or accepting the point of view the teacher is trying to get across. "I don't understand." "Isn't there another way of looking at that?" "I know what you are trying to say, but it's hard for me to deal with that." These are the kinds of statements that most teachers will see not as a threat to their authority but as an opportunity to teach.

With teachers, as with all people, we shouldn't expect too much. Teachers are human beings too. They have the same fears and faults and failings as others have. Some days things just don't go right for them. Sometimes they have problems at home they have to worry about or difficulties with other staff people that might be on their minds. They may have meant to prepare better for that particular class, but just ran out of time. They may want to be more patient, but just can't seem to deal with any more hassles on that particular day.

That's not to say that it's right for teachers to take out their frustrations on their students. It certainly isn't fair for any adult to make young people pay for troubles that are not their fault.

Teachers fail. They get mixed up and make mistakes. They don't always get it right. More than anything else they probably need a kind word and our understanding and forgiveness when they mess up—just like we all do.

That might be an interesting thing to try. Instead of accusing or blaming or complaining, you might try complimenting a teacher, encouraging him, and building him up. You might try saying something helpful in class or thanking him for what he's done for the class.

You never know. That affirmed and supported teacher might just feel good enough about himself and what is going on in class to admit that he's wrong the next time he makes a mistake.

Why am I afraid of spiders? When I'm so big and spiders are so little, why am I afraid of them? Why am I afraid of everything?

 Fear is something like red pepper in chili. A little bit is a good thing. Too much, and you might as well throw the chili out. A little fear works for us. Too much, and it can ruin our life.

God meant fear to help us. Most of the time it does. Fear helps our body get ready to protect itself in times of danger. Even without thinking about it, when we are afraid, our body gets ready to fight or to run away. We breathe faster; our senses seem to get sharper; and when we are powered by some stuff called adrenaline, we can move quicker, run faster, and jump higher than we ever could if we were not afraid.

You've probably heard stories about how people have done superhuman things when they're afraid. A woman moved a car off her injured child. A man jumped over an 11-foot fence. There is no way either of them could have normally done those things. Because of fear, they were able to do what was necessary to save themselves or the person they loved.

Fear is not fun. The sense of terror that makes our heart beat in our mouth and our head start to swim is not the kind of experience we would look for. In fact, we do everything we can to stay away from things that make us afraid. Though there is a certain "high" in being "scared to death" (look at the popularity of the horror movie and the roller coaster), we generally do what we can to avoid being frightened.

We cannot avoid some fear situations, and some of them are very hard to endure. We wait our turn to make a speech. Our hands are clammy; we feel like we're going to faint; we have to just about hang onto our feet to keep them from running out the door. We'd do almost anything to avoid that kind of fear. That fear is "normal," and we "live with it."

Everyone is afraid. Even the biggest macho bully in the school is afraid sometimes. Some people are better at hiding their fear than others, and some can tolerate more fear than others—

but everyone is afraid. Some show their fear; some hide it. Some hide in drugs or alcohol, trying to escape their fears, but since fear really is inside us, we cannot run away from it.

For all of its unpleasantness, most of the time we deal with fear fairly well. We might blush a little or begin to perspire. We might get sweaty palms and feel a little light-headed, but we survive the fearful situation—live through the speech or find some way to stay away from the one who is always pushing us around. In some way we deal with our fears.

Some fears, however, are completely irrational. They are called phobias—but calling them that doesn't make them any easier to live with. They are like fears gone wild or like fears that have taken on a personality of their own. They are huge things— mean and unpredictable, and they're very hard to deal with.

There are all kinds of phobias. Everyone probably has to deal with some kind of a phobia at some time in his or her life. So they certainly aren't rare. The most common phobias are ones like claustrophobia—the fear of closed places; acrophobia—the fear of heights; or agoraphobia—the fear of open spaces. And there are dozens of others.

The one thing that is alike about all of these is that phobias are a fear reaction that is way out of proportion to the danger that triggers them. Panic is excessive fear caused by a phobia.

A person who is suffering from claustrophobia is in real trouble when he is in a tight place, a small room, or a closed area. He may feel that he's going to faint, that he can't breathe, or that the walls are closing in. He becomes terrified—almost out of control. He turns white and breathes hard; you can see terror in his eyes.

That same kind of panic can be brought on by many other things. For some it is even caused by tiny things like spiders or mice; some can't handle chickens or birds. Others can't stand crowds or noise. Whatever it is—the reaction is the same: sheer, stark terror.

Phobias can last a long time. Some people suffer with them for years. They learn to deal with the fear by staying away from the thing that makes them afraid. A friend of mine—a big, strong man—cannot stand heights. When he took a trip to the mountains, he spent the whole time riding in the back seat with a bag over his head while his wife drove. It did absolutely no good whatsoever to point out to him that his reaction was absurd, completely silly by some standards. He was terrified. Needless to say, he does not go up in the mountains anymore.

Similarly, you will find people who avoid crowds, anything having to do with insects or snakes, high buildings, flying, and so on—just because they are trying to control their phobias.

The reason why we suffer from these extreme fears is not clear—even to psychologists. Some say that they reflect emotional confusion—some other kind of a fear that is being focused on a single thing in the environment. Still others think the phobia is caused by a chemical imbalance. Others think it is a way we have of dealing with inner conflict. In any case, it is not likely that anyone will be able to tell just what makes us afraid of spiders, speed, heights, or anything else. It is just one of those things that happen to us. We have to learn to deal with the fear.

That is not to say that professionals cannot help us with our phobias and fears if we need help. The worst thing we can do with our fears is to try to hide them. It may seem a bit embarrassing to admit that a spider can throw us into a complete panic or that we have to put a bag over our head to stand on the top of a building, but pretending the fear is not there will do nothing at all to make it go away. It may, in fact, make it worse.

Psychologists and counselors can help with phobias by working with us to understand what lies behind our fears and teaching us ways to overcome them gradually. So it's important to take those fears to a counselor when our life is being interfered with by our fears, when we find we cannot do what we want to anymore, or when we are being controlled by our fears. Then it is time to face the fears, deal with them, and get help.

One elderly woman was so overcome by her fear of the outdoors that it soon became impossible for her to leave her house. She had to have someone do her shopping for her, and she did everything else by phone. When a fear becomes that consuming, it's time to get help for it.

For most of us, even our phobias are relatively mild. We avoid the spiders or scream a little when we see them. We stand back from the railing at the edge of the cliff, and we shake our head a little to get over the dizziness when we are in too tight a place. We learn to live with our fears.

Tolerance to fear is an individual thing. Just as some people are physically stronger, some are emotionally better able to deal with pressures, problems, and fears. Telling ourselves we ought to be stronger when we are terrified is about as effective as telling ourselves we ought to be physically stronger when we're trying to lift 500 pounds. Chances are, in either case, all the telling will only make us feel more like a failure because we cannot do what we expect of ourselves.

Fear is nothing to be ashamed of. Even what seem like silly fears are not foolish. They are real. They can cause a great deal of pain, and we do best when we deal with them and get the necessary help.

God gave us fear as a way to protect ourselves in danger. When fear, because of sin, goes astray and interferes with our life, we need to seek help to make that fear manageable again.

What are the boundaries of premarital sex? Is it all right to touch someone sexually?

 Sometimes adults want both to control and protect teens. Their answer to a question like "What are the bounds of premarital sex?" might be: "Don't do it!" Similarly, they would give a flat no to the question about sexually touching someone.

Though these answers might be simple, they aren't very helpful, especially when you are alone with someone you really care about, someone you've come to love very much. When he or she wants to touch you or kiss you, words like "they told me to say no" really don't help much.

But, on the other hand, we know that there is something special about sex—all of it. From sexual attraction to sexual intercourse, it is something unique. For human beings sex is not just a convenient mating activity (as it is for animals), nor is it mutual exercise (as some would have us believe).

Sex is a gift of God that has both the power to create and to destroy—a gift that can be the most beautiful thing two people can do together, or simply something dirty, sinful, and foolish. The task we have as responsible children of God is to know the difference and to know how to use our sexuality as He would have us use it.

The first step in that right use is understanding what sex is. For animals it is simply a physical act. For human beings sex is also a physical act, but it is more. It is a language, a way of "saying" something. It is a special way of telling our feelings.

A kiss, for example, may communicate many things. A peck on the cheek says something about affection, or at least attention. A kiss between two people in love says something important about how they feel about each other—says it in a way that words cannot speak. That one kiss says more than a million words about how important that other person is, how much he or she means, how close the two people are—and many other things.

All "sexual" activity is really a language. A touch says something. The person doing the touching means it to say something.

The person touched receives that touch—and the meaning behind it. Even a look can have a great deal more meaning than the simple meeting of two people's eyes.

Sexual intercourse then, whatever you call it in the teen slang of the day, is more than two people mating. The act of intercourse itself is a part of that language of sex. It says what a kiss does, but in a more special and more important way. It says in a way that is unique to that act: "We are one." By this God-given act, this special way of coming together reserved only for two people who are in love and committed to each other, this unique way of touching, and of being a part of each other, we are saying something about our unity as two people that cannot be said in any other way. By this act we are one. We have bound ourselves together—and if it produces a child, as one we will accept that child and remain together to raise and love and care for that product of our love.

That's why sexual intercourse is reserved for marriage. It is not set apart just because some older people think that young people are not ready, or because they have made a lot of rules to keep teens on their toes. It is because in the language of love, God has given that special act as the one way human beings have of expressing the kind of oneness that only comes when two people, blessed by God, commit themselves to each other for a lifetime. Any other use of that gift is wrong.

Suppose sexual intercourse becomes the convenient end of every date. What does it mean then? When it becomes as common as a handshake, it means nothing at all. It has been robbed of its voice. It can say nothing other than, "I am interested in you, excited by you." It is a meaningless act done for no reason. It is empty.

Worse, if sexual intercourse is the expected end of every brief encounter between two people, what is left to communicate the kind of special love that comes only rarely in a lifetime and that is indeed meant to last a lifetime? What language does it have left? How can its specialness be spoken? How, other than in empty words, can that special love come to life? Robbed of its voice, it has no means of expression. And that voiceless love, no matter how special it may seem, will die for lack of a way to share it.

Each step of our relationship with that other person has a language all its own. Think of how you "fall in love." First you are interested, then attracted, then infatuated; then the love starts to mature: you care about the other person, begin to put him first, and feel a genuine affection beyond that for others—even members of your family. Then you are willing to make a commitment to him—something that might even last a lifetime. Then, when you are ready, when the love has grown, when the commitment is sure—you are willing to become one with him both in marriage and in sexual union.

Each of those steps has its own physical "language." Attention often is expressed in a look, interest by the touch of a hand, affection or infatuation by a kiss—or even more. Each expression is appropriate to the kind of love that produces it.

God is sometimes seen as a "crabby old Father" making difficult rules for us—rules about "adultery" and keeping ourselves "chaste." In reality He is trying to help us deal with a very important and special gift. He wants the love that we find with another person to be so great as to be nearly perfect—so special that we'll be willing to build our lives on it. He wants it to be the finest thing that happens in our life. He wants that so much that He has given a special language to our love. The language is called sex—and no other human relationship has a similar way of expressing its specialness.

What are the bounds of premarital sex? What are you trying to say by what you are doing in any given situation?

Is the kiss in the back seat saying something about love, or is it saying something else? Is it an expression of caring for that other person, or is it a way of making ourselves feel better? Is it a special gift to that other person or a kind of taking from him or her—a taking that only gratifies ourself?

Is it right to touch—or even to go beyond that? What is the touch saying? What is its purpose? Is the touch a gift or something taken? Is the touch an expression of love or something for self? Is it done out of caring for the other person or in order to get something?

No rules will cover every kind of touch or embrace that you might find yourself involved in. It is impossible to say when and if you might hold hands, how long a kiss is supposed to last with this person or that, even where and when you can touch another person.

Recognizing that sex is basically a way of saying love to another person, it should do that. If the touch, the kiss, or the embrace does not say love, but says something else, it is a taking instead of a giving. If it doesn't really matter who that other person is—then it is wrong because then sex is being used for self, for taking instead of giving, for personal gratification instead of as a gift to a loved person.

The test isn't always easy to apply. The heat of the moment tends to take over. There are lots of difficulties in trying to use sex in a responsible, God-pleasing way. Remembering that it is a gift of God helps. Remembering that it is meant to be a gift of love for another person helps too.

Lots of frustrations, problems, and confusion will arise for you as you work out your love and commitment to others—especially for that one special other. But God has promised to help you and to bless you as you "fall in love" and seek to express that special love to that other person.

His love covers many mistakes, and His forgiveness recreates when sex does not say what we want it to say, or when our expression of love is not what we meant it to be.

His most important gift is His constant and forgiving love in Jesus Christ that helps us become not a problem to others we love but a blessing and a gift to them.

Q

Why are stepparents so tough to get along with?

A

I wonder what your stepparent would say if we asked him or her the same question. Maybe the response would sound something like this: "Me? Me tough to get along with! Let me tell you something; I'm a regular cream puff compared to my stepchild. That kid is impossible. Everything I do for her is wrong. Every move I make is wrong. If I say anything, it's the wrong thing. If I say nothing—I should have said something. I can't win. And even when I try to be nice, what do I get in return? More complaining, more yelling, and more demands. Me tough? I could tell you a thing or two about tough to get along with."

The stepparent-stepchild relationship seems to be made for frustration, misunderstanding, mistrust—and breakdown. Almost everything works against it. It is the rare stepparent or child who makes it work.

Think of the potential for disaster in this relationship. From your point of view as the stepchild, you have this "other" adult who has seemingly invaded the family. You didn't invite him in. You weren't even consulted. Just all of a sudden, there's this person living in the house who acts a lot like a father but seems to be doing it all wrong.

After all, this one is nothing like the original. He's always saying the wrong thing, always criticizing, always expecting too much, and always griping. He's not like your real father, who (at least in your memory) tried to do the right thing. He cared. This new guy doesn't even seem to care.

There is the real problem. Stepparents and children are usually put into the parent-child relationship before the people involved know each other, much less care about each other or trust each other.

As the child, you couldn't care less about someone who wants to take your father's place. That may be the last thing you are looking for—and as a result, you are all set not to care about this new person.

Meanwhile, your stepfather is so busy working at his relationship with a new wife that he doesn't have the time to work at the relationship with his new stepchild.

Even in something as simple as discipline or criticism from parent to child, the stepparent-stepchild relationship is in trouble. If we are willing to accept (even though we don't always like it) criticism or scolding or punishment from our parents, it is because we feel that they are doing it for our own good—because they love us, they are trying to help us learn to deal with life better, or learn better habits, or avoid trouble, or something. We may not agree with what they say, but because we share a mutual love and respect, we can at least accept it.

With a stepparent, that mutual caring often is not there. His criticism seems selfish; his punishment seems cruel; his scolding seems like vicious yelling. There is no way we can accept what our stepparent has done. As a result we probably end up yelling back. And that sounds like hatred and rejection to our stepparent, who simply takes that outburst as additional evidence that we don't really care anyway.

There is no easy way to make the stepparent-stepchild relationship work. If it is going to work, it will take a lot of care and attention from both people involved. As stepchildren we will have to:

1. Recognize that this new parent will never be "just like" our former parent. She will have strengths and weaknesses, pluses and minuses, things we like and things we don't like. We need God's help to accept that person as she is and not expect her to change to become like we want her to be.

2. Learn to accept the stepparent as a real parent. Shutting him out, resenting his presence, acting as though he were an intruder, biting back in anger—all of those things will only make the situation worse. We will want to seek God's help to understand and accept the new parent.

3. Get love started. It won't be easy. It is much easier to hate someone, to turn our back on someone, to find fault with someone, and to reject someone. It is much easier to find reasons why we are right and the other person is wrong—to draw ourselves up and say, "I'll never apologize. She can just come

crawling back to me." But all of that will get us nowhere, in spite of failings and faults and whatever problems there have been in the past. In spite of the fact that your stepparent may have ignored you or insulted you or treated you badly, you will want to seek God's help to reach out to that parent in love. Give back kindness where there has been anger. Give back caring where you have discovered criticism. Give something of yourself where you have found only taking.

It's a tall order. It is never easy to love—especially to love someone who seems so unlovable—but most stepparents really want to be loved. They want to do well as a parent. They want to be helpful if they have a chance.

The next time you feel like yelling, the next time you are the one who has been hurt, the one who has been slighted, or the one who has to pay the price—instead of yelling, give a hug, a small gift, or a kind word. You'd be surprised how a thing like that can get something started that just might make the whole situation better for everyone.

The greatest gift God has given us is forgiveness in His Son Jesus Christ. Without that forgiveness none of us would have a chance of being "right" with God—or with each other.

That make-it-new-and-right-again forgiveness is God's gift to us—the gift we have to share with others, even with stepparents.

Q *Why do parents always make you feel guilty?*

A Making someone feel guilty is a very effective way to get that person to do what you want, and guilt is rather easy to start in most people.

Of course, there are some who have lost touch with their ability to feel guilt. They literally "have no regrets" about almost anything they do. They're not very nice people to be around. They take things, hurt people, and seem to care for no one but themselves. The rest of us feel guilty when we've broken a rule—especially if it caused someone else some pain.

We've all been there. Let's say we've had a fight with a friend. Maybe it wasn't a very important fight, but we said a few things in the heat of the moment. And when we thought about it later, we felt terrible. Not only did we hurt our friend with our words, but we let ourselves down by getting mad again when we meant not to. Then we wish we could take it back, do it over, and somehow escape from the finger that seems to be pointing at us. That's guilt.

Guilt feels so bad that we'd do almost anything to get rid of it. That's what makes forgiveness—especially God's forgiveness—so great. He's not just patting us on the head and telling us to make the best of our pain, or that things will some day be better. He is offering us forgiveness in Jesus Christ that can take the hurt and the guilt away.

That doesn't mean that guilt cannot still bother us, drag us down, or be used against us. Parents and others know how to use it. Maybe they learned from us.

Many children know how to use guilt on their parents:
"Everyone else's parents are letting them go." Hidden message:
Don't you feel bad? You are the only heartless and cruel parents in the whole school.
"I never get to do anything like that." Hidden message: Don't you feel guilty? Other parents who really love their kids let them do what they want to, at least occasionally.
"If I don't get some new clothes (that new outfit, those new shoes,

whatever), I will be so completely out of it that everyone will think I come from the hills or something." Hidden message: Aren't you afraid other parents will find out how little you care about your children?

And so it goes. In each case the hidden message is meant to make our parents feel so guilty that they will do what we want them to. That's using guilt. Most parents don't want to use guilt to get their way. They don't set out to do that. But it works so well.

Your mother says, "Clean your room."

You say, "Not now. It can wait."

Your mother has several options. She can wait and see if the job gets done later. Or she can "persuade" you to do it now.

If she decides to try to persuade you, she has several more options. She can threaten: "Do it, or else." But she may not want a fight and may not know exactly what the "or else" would be.

She can nag or beg: "Please do it now. I need to have the house cleaned up today because we have company coming tomorrow."

Or she can use guilt. "I've been slaving all day for you; I've washed your clothes, done the dishes, and cleaned the whole house. All I ask you to do is one simple thing, and you're too busy or too lazy. Doesn't it mean anything to you that your father and I work our fingers to the bone for you?"

Well, which one will work best? Probably the guilt routine.

Similarly, parents can use guilt to try to keep us faithful to their rules when they aren't around: "Of course, you are not like those others who are always getting in trouble. It is so nice to have a child who is an example for others to follow instead of one who follows others into all kinds of trouble." Meanwhile, you may be feeling like something less than a shining example for the world to follow—and as a result you feel guilty again.

So guilt works. It does get us to do things we don't necessarily want to do, and it pushes us to obey the rules, even when we don't particularly see the purpose of the rule.

But guilt is dangerous as well. It is possible to get a guilt overload. If all you hear is how you messed up, or how you ought to be better, and all you feel is guilty about what you have done and about what you have not done, you can burn out the circuits—get guilt overload and just give up. A person with guilt overload says, "Well, I'm never going to get it right anyway, no matter how hard I try—so why even try?"

Sometimes parents call a person with guilt overload "rebellious." The reason a teen says no or doesn't even try anymore may not be rebellion. It may just be that he has given up and is trying to get out from under an overload of guilt. If your parents are really into the guilt thing, it would be best to talk to them about it.

Some people think that what makes families "Christian" is that everyone in the family is so good. They seem to think that Christian families at least pretend always to get along, help each other, and be kind. Most of them find that picture understandably phoney.

Christians are not people playing at being saints. Christians are forgiven people who are in the business of forgiving. Sometimes the most important words we can exchange are "I'm sorry." And the response is "I forgive you." This should not be just an exchange of words—but a setting aside of a hurt or an obstacle that threatens to do real damage to the relationships in the home. And then, by the grace of God in Jesus, the hurt is forgiven. It is gone. It doesn't have to be brought up again.

So in a Christian home, the one thing we can't really use very effectively is guilt—because the guilt is forgiven. At least, it is supposed to be.

Your best approach might be to schedule a long talk for all concerned to help all see what they are doing to each other when they use guilt to try to get their way. That kind of communication might go a long way toward helping real Christian love become a greater part of your home.

In the meantime, the best thing to do with guilt is to get rid of it. If you feel guilty about something, say so. Tell the person who is hurt by what you did about how you feel. Ask for forgiveness. And the guilt is gone.

Sidestep the phoney guilt, the manipulative guilt, the "poor me" kind of guilt that some people always want to give out.

Faced by someone who says, "Don't you feel sorry for me and want to do something for me?" the Christian says, "Not sorry. I feel joyful that in Christ the sin that has dragged you down is forgiven and that the power of God can make you new."

It won't be easy to avoid the guilt. If you can act first and show love first, maybe there won't be a reason for your parents or others to try out their guilt on you.

Q *Why won't my parents accept my friends who are different?*

A Though they probably won't admit it, your parents are a little afraid of you. If you pressed them, they'd say that they have always been. Oh, they're not really afraid you'll hurt them, at least not physically. They're afraid that somehow, for all their good intentions and earnest efforts, you'll just turn out wrong.

There must have been a time when being a parent was easier—at least more natural. Back when families pioneered on the frontier—when no one was even sure they'd live till next year, much less get anything that looked like a luxury—parents didn't have much time to worry about how they were treating their children, disciplining them, and molding them. Parents tended to expect children to cook, clean, sew, work the fields, or do whatever needed doing to help the family survive.

Things are different now. Few families are in a survival mode. Parents have been told a million times that what their children become depends pretty much on what they do with them. If a child "goes wrong"—as people say—everyone immediately assumes that his parents beat the poor kid or locked him in the closet or failed to love him—did something that made him turn into a social misfit or worse. As a result, parents stand paralyzed at the thought that one of their children might go bad. The fear is so intense that some parents actually freeze up. "What should I do now?" they are constantly asking themselves and others. They read books and listen to lectures, trying to learn how to do the thing that will guarantee that their child will turn out OK.

Well, all of that worry probably makes the job of raising children all that much more difficult when the children are young, and nearly impossible when children become teens.

When children are very young, there usually is not much that easily gets between a parent and a child. A child is largely shaped by what happens at home—by parents' attitudes and affection, attention and direction. Children interact with people outside of the

94

family, but don't seem to be greatly influenced by what goes on outside of the home.

That makes the worrisome parenting job a little easier. If it is true that the child has to be shaped and molded, then having some control over what the child does, thinks, and even feels gives the parents some influence on the child.

Then the child becomes a teenager. If parents were scared before, a teenage child produces sheer terror. How in the world are you going to be sure a child doesn't rebel, do something stupid, run away, or whatever if you can't control what the child does and thinks and especially the kinds of people he or she associates with?

As a child grows into the teen years, it quickly becomes apparent that this person who once lived and breathed what she was told by her parents and who most willingly tried to please them at every turn is becoming her own person. She has her own ideas, thoughts, and opinions, and these don't always agree with those of her parents.

She may believe that a certain rock group is "awesome." Her parents may think the group is the pits. She may think the clothes she recently purchased are "the greatest." Her parents may think they look like something salvaged from a fire sale. She may think the posters on her wall are—and on and on it goes.

Very soon parents begin to feel that they are losing control. How will they be able to insure that their child will not run amuck and cause them all kinds of grief and embarrassment? They are aware that they are no longer the greatest influence in their child's life. They are losing their place to her friends, to her schoolmates—to her "peers," as the counselors say.

Slowly it begins to dawn on parents that they won't be able to keep their teen away from the influence of peers—of those others out there who seem to make her decisions, set her values, influence her likes and dislikes, make up her mind, and all the rest.

Well, if they can't stop the influence of peers, the next thing a worried parent might do is try to control the others who are having an influence on their child.

Obviously, there are a lot of dangerous young people out there—at least from a parent's point of view. There are those in the midst of open rebellion. Look at the way they wear their hair. Look at their clothes. Look at the kinds of cars they drive—and at what they do or don't do with their spare time. There are druggies out there, drunks, kids who run away from home, and all other kinds of bad kids.

Now if it is true that their child is being influenced by peers and if some of those peers are less than desirable in life-style, habits, attitudes, and the like, it might be of paramount importance to keep their child away from these freaks, weirdos, rejects, burnouts, and the like. As a result, parents find themselves making rules about the kids their child can hang around with and those they think it necessary to avoid.

"You'd better just stay away from him."

"But why, Mom? I like the guy."

"He's just not the kind of person you ought to be associating with. Look for other friends—kids more . . . more . . . well, more like you, if you know what I mean."

"But I don't know what you mean."

And so the discussion goes.

There probably isn't a lot you are going to be able to do to convince your parents that the punkers, burnouts, and others are the right kind of folks to have as friends. They look at things like hair styles and make decisions about the desirability of this or that person on appearance or reputation. That may not seem fair. People who are afraid aren't always either reasonable or fair. You may have to live with their fears, at least for a time.

Of course, there are things you can do to help them with their fears. First of all, you might let them know that you understand why they are afraid and try to give them some reassurance. Show them that you are not planning to become a heathen, run away from home, or turn into a convicted felon. If they can see that you are still living by the sense of right and wrong that they tried to teach you, they will much less likely fall victim to the our-kid-is-going-straight-down-the-drain overreaction.

Second, you might choose your friends very carefully. It just may be that your folks have a point about some kids. Some, especially those who are really gone on themselves, are very good at taking attention from others—and taking anything else they can get their hands on, without a thought for the person doing the giving. You might not want to be the one taken from and taken advantage of. Real friends give as much as they take. Look for such friends.

Third, be patient with your folks. Try not to get mad at them about their rules that seem silly, about the times they seem to treat you like you are still eight years old, and about the nagging they do. Try to understand where they are coming from. Try to understand their fear and give them some kind words of gratitude—at least gratitude for the fact that they love you and care about what happens to you. The more "adult" you are in your reaction, the more likely they are to treat you in an adult way the next time a conflict comes up. When you throw a fit, yell, call names, slam the door, and the like—it just doesn't give your folks much confidence in you, in your contention that you have grown up, and in your ability to function like an adult.

Last, give them reason to trust you. Be responsible. Try to set their fears aside. Call when you are late. Share your plans for the evening. Explain what you are doing and why. Introduce your friends to them. Give them the benefit of the doubt on a slightly overbearing rule. Show them that you can associate with the less than desirable and, instead of suffering great damage from the bad influence of others, you can have a positive influence on some of those who are indeed lost, confused, and rebellious.

Most of all, don't expect your parents to change overnight. It took them years to perfect their worries; they heard and believed so many warnings—and they want the best for you so much that they can't pat you on the head and send you out there without warnings, rules, and restrictions—at least not yet.

In time they may make it. Trusting someone takes a lot of practice. Some married people don't ever manage to learn to trust. Trust is fostered by trustworthiness and destroyed by irresponsibility and carelessness. It might be tough, but your freedom to make your own choices and pick your own friends may only come with time and with practice on your part.

Is it wrong to want to be the best?

 I'm sure the year 1959 doesn't mean much to you. I'm just as sure that names like Nellie Fox, Luis Aparicio, and Jim Landis don't make your heart throb either. They do mine, though.

I was 12 years old in 1959, growing up in Chicago. It was the year that the Chicago White Sox won the American League championship. They hadn't done it for 40 years, and they haven't done it since.

Anyway, it was also in 1959 that I came up to my dad with one of those autograph books that used to be really big with junior high kids. You had your family, best friends, and anyone else you could grab write something in the book and sign it. Usually, they wrote deep, lasting sentiments like "You're neat" or "Have fun" or "Roses are red / Violets are blue / If Lutherans are smart / What happened to you?"

But back to my dad. I remember standing there, waiting as he wrote his little message and signed it with a flair. You know what he wrote? I still have the book. This was his message:

To the star pitcher of the 1975 Chicago White Sox
From his dad—with love

I'll tell you, he couldn't have written anything at that time in my life to bring me more joy and pride. I don't know if he really thought I ever had a chance, but back then I did. I really did. I thought I might pitch for the White Sox. I tried that year and in the years following to be the best ballplayer I could.

Then came 1975. Maybe you can guess. By 1975, I had already been cut from the college baseball team. The year came and went, and the White Sox never called—naturally. I have to tell you, though; I never once thought of my dad's message that whole year. By 1975, I had developed other interests, had other goals, and was chasing them. I was still playing baseball in 1975, but with church teams, and we never once got TV coverage.

Looking back, I can see how the Lord taught me something in all of that. I didn't know He was teaching it to me at the time. I remember how much it hurt not to see my name on the roster for the baseball team. Along the way, though, I learned that you can strive to be the best, work at it, dig in and go for it, fail, and still have a life that's rich and full and meaningful.

Now you want to know if it's OK to want to be the best. Let me respond by giving you a few "as long as" statements. It's OK to want to be the best

- as long as you don't hurt others or yourself along the way;
- as long as you're willing to accept failure if it comes;
- as long as being "the best" means doing the best you can with your gifts;
- as long as in striving to be the best you don't have to compromise your faith and your values;
- as long as your reason for wanting to be the best is to bring God glory;
- as long as you're able to find contentment and peace in your Lord and not in your own achievements.

That's quite a list, isn't it? I suppose the list helps you see how cautious you have to be when trying to do your best. The track record for those who reach star status holding the rest of their life together is not very good. Just try and keep up, for instance, with who's married and who isn't in Hollywood.

Remember a few years ago how well the film *Chariots of Fire* presented the challenge to Christian achievers? An Olympic runner refused to run on Sunday because his church taught that Sunday was to be a day of total rest, dedicated to worshiping the Lord. He simply would not run! Nobody could understand it, but he knew that his values came first and his goal of being the best second.

Col. 3:17 says, "And whatever you do, in word or deed, do everything in the name of the Lord Jesus, giving thanks to God the Father through Him." For any achiever seeking to do his or her best, that's a great verse. It helps us to check our motivation. It also keeps up front just who gets the praise for the success we achieve. I think it would look good on a locker door or maybe, better, it would work great for a team motto or a personal verse to whisper just before a test or a race or a competition.

I think that the greatest danger in striving to be the best

comes when you begin to realize that you may not win the gold (that 1975 is coming, and it's not looking good at all). Some people just can't handle the thought of failing. I heard an Olympic skater recently talk about how before the Winter Olympics she felt that her whole life was riding on her four minutes on the ice. Then she fell, and it seemed as if her life ended the second she hit the ice. It took months, she said, before she could even think about skating again. She believed that she had failed her parents, her coach, her nation, and herself.

That's the danger—that she might never have put skates on again or seen herself as gifted. For Christians, this is where faith becomes so important. For us, real contentment, the one thing that keeps us going and fulfilled and happy is always there for us—always! We believe that God loves us, that to Him we are always No. 1. Christ has won that status for us. No wonder, Paul could write: "I have learned, in whatever state I am [win, lose, or draw], to be content" (Phil. 4:11).

Waiting for you at the end of your life on earth is a crown that's reserved for winners just like you. Jesus Himself promised it when He said, "Be faithful unto death, and I will give you the crown of life" (Rev. 2:10). The word He used there for "crown" in the original Greek language is *stephanos*. If you know anyone named Stephen, now you know what his name means. A "stephanos" was the laurel wreath reserved for the winner of an athletic event in the ancient Olympic games. That's what your Lord promises you, and as long as you keep that image in front of you, of your Lord awarding you a crown of life, things will be just fine.

One last thing. Striving for excellence is something Christians do. Some of the people who have done the most in the history of civilization have been Christians. Maybe it's because we know how to succeed and how to fail. Maybe Christians are good strivers because we're so affected by heaven—something out ahead of us, something good, perfect, beautiful, and true, pulling us always toward the good, the better, and the best. It was said of Jesus, "He does all things well." No one will ever say that about me or about you. We'll try. Sometimes we'll finish first. Sometimes we'll finish last. Sometimes we won't even finish. Because we do it for Him, though, it's all worth it.

I'm not so sure I would have wanted to pitch for the White Sox anyway—certainly not in 1975. They had a lousy season. OK. Right. Be honest. I know—you're right. I would have loved to have pitched for the White Sox. I wonder. Are there baseball teams in heaven?

Q *Why does suicide sometimes seem the only way out?*

A My all-time favorite movie is titled *It's a Wonderful Life*. The movie has been out since 1946, but whenever I see that it's about to hit the late late show, I put the popcorn on and stay up to watch it.

Jimmy Stewart plays a character named George in the movie. George is in real trouble. Financially and almost every other way, his life seems to be falling apart. He begins believing that he's worth more dead than alive. So George decides to commit suicide.

Then comes Clarence, a chubby angel sent by God to save George's life and win his wings in the process. (By the way, you'll never find anything in the Bible about an angel named Clarence or about angels winning wings. Anyway . . .) Clarence takes George on a tour of Bedford Falls, his hometown. He has George see what the lives of others would have been like had he never lived. One by one, George sees how his life affected his family and his friends, how they were changed and enriched by his having lived.

George decides to live, not just to live, but to celebrate being alive. Clarence, by the way, gets his wings, and I'm left crying sentimental tears into my handkerchief again.

One thing you learn from George in *It's a Wonderful Life* is this: you can be a regular, everyday person and still think about suicide. It happens. Those thoughts of suicide come. They even come to Christians.

I had a Christian teacher once who took her own life. I knew a mother of five who committed suicide. I've known a straight A high school student who killed himself. I've known a pastor, too, and a grandfather, and a church organist, and a farmer, and a wealthy business executive. They all, tragically, chose dying over living.

Some of the latest statistics I've seen on suicide show what a terrible threat it is. Look at these:

Once every minute someone in the United States attempts suicide.

Three Americans take their lives every hour of every day.
In the past decade the suicide rate for Americans under the age of 30 has increased 300 percent.

I can tell by your question that you may have considered suicide to be a way out for yourself. That means you've probably struggled with some haunting and destructive feelings. When people consider suicide, they may be struggling with one or several of these feelings:

- I'm lonely, and no one seems to care.
- I'm worthless, no good to anyone.
- I've lost all hope. It will never get better.
- I can't measure up to what others expect of me or to what I expect of myself.
- I can't put together this failed relationship.
- I am unloved.

Those feelings, backed up by fact or not, are the stuff of which nightmares are made—and suicides. It's for those reasons that people try to end their own lives and often succeed.

If I could say anything to someone thinking about suicide, I'd want to say these six words: *the best way out is always through!* I believe that. Suicide may be a way out of hurt and pain and struggle, but it is never the *best* way out. The best way out is through.

In the Bible, you'll find a very special word that captures this principle. The word gets translated in the New Testament sometimes as "endurance" and at other times as "steadfastness." In the original language of the New Testament the word in Greek is actually *hupomone*. It really means "to remain under." You know, if I had another child, I'd consider naming that child "Hupomone." I like the word that much. Of course, little "Hupie" wouldn't ever talk to me, but *hupomone* is a great word. It means to remain under a burden, to hang tough, to stay strong, to stand firm, to stay put and tough it out without giving in.

You can remember *hupomone* by thinking of a hippo and a pocketful of money. If you'd like to see the word at work in the Scriptures, check out Rom. 5:1—5; Heb. 10:35—36; and Rev. 14:12.

You see, it's a word like *hupomone* that reminds us of some great truths we have as Christians. For instance:
We can make it through anything because we have Christ with us
     and in us to pull us through.
We are surrounded by people in the church who care about us
     and will be there to support us.
We have hope not in ourselves but in an all-powerful Lord, who
     loves us and will never hurt us or ask us to endure more than
     we can handle victoriously.
Scripture verses like Phil. 4:10—13; Rom. 15:1—2; and 1 Cor. 10:13 provide some real strength to people wondering about a way out. Each passage supports the idea that going through really tough times may be the very time in our lives when we finally and fully learn what it means to believe and to hope and to hang on to a dream.

That's what I want for you. If I could order up a chubby little angel named Clarence to convince you, I would. The Bible, though, is more than enough. It says that you're worth everything to your Lord. The whole Bible story is a story of God working in history to make your life full and complete. God isn't through with you yet. I'm sure of that. If He were through with you, He'd take you home to heaven with Him now. Your name isn't Elijah, though, and you'd better not plan on a fiery chariot. Instead, there's life with all its hard knocks, hurt feelings, and dark days and darker nights, but through it all, the same Lord who loved you enough to die for you will be there for you. I believe that. I hope you do, too.

Now it may be that you have a concern for someone who might be considering suicide. Experts in suicide prevention would want you to ask yourself these questions that signal a possible suicide attempt: Has there been any sudden change in the person's personality? Does the person talk about suicide? Has there been a recent crisis in the person's life? Have you noticed any physical symptoms like an extreme weight loss or sleepless nights? Is the person severely depressed? Has the person ever actually attempted suicide?

Questions like these will help you decide if suicide may be something a friend is considering. You can get other help from a suicide prevention hotline, a professional counselor, or a pastor.

But be a friend. If you're really concerned, do something about it now. It may mean time. It may also mean a chance to be a Clarence in your own right. For *every* George, there must be a Clarence, especially in the church.

And don't forget *hupomone!* The best way out is always through!

Q How do I know what's true and what isn't?

 A Let me introduce you to "Dear Hal." Hal is one of those advice givers like Dear Abby. He's always there with some little gem of wisdom in answer to your questions. Hal's word is truth to a lot of people because, well, just because Hal is Hal.

Here's a little sample of Hal's advice.

Dear Hal:

My parents are really on my case lately. I can't stand it. I'm angry and ready to quit the whole scene. What should I do?

Signed,
Locked in My Room

Dear Locked in My Room

I don't know whether you're locked in your room from the inside or from the outside. Did those nasty parents of yours lock you up, or have you locked them out? Who cares, I guess. What's important is that you're in your room away from those out-of-date, tired old bores. If I were you, I'd stockpile food in my room, put the stereo on full blast, and cut off all lines of communication with the old folks at home. Pout and get bitter. That's my advice. Sooner or later, they'll come crawling to your door on their knees, begging you to come out. Don't—at least not until you have to.

Your friend,
Hal

Some guy, huh? Hal always has something to say. Here's one more example:

Dear Hal:

I made the team, but it looks as if I'll be riding the bench all season. What a bummer! I think I'll quit rather than be so humiliated. What do you think?

Signed,
Bench-Warmer

Dear Bench-Warmer:

Quit the team. They'll lose without you. Frankly, they would have lost with you anyway. The coach stinks. His judgment is lousy. The team stinks. The school stinks. You stink, too. You're a failure, Bench-Warmer. Everybody doesn't have to know it, though. Quit now, and you may come out smelling like a rose.

Your friend,
Hal

Just one more. Read Hal's great advice to a guy who thinks he's on the edge of something wonderful:

Dear Hal:

There's this girl in chemistry class. She's unbelievably good-looking and nice, too. I haven't said a word to her yet. To be honest, I'm sorta afraid. What should I do?

Signed,
Cold Feet

Dear Cold Feet:

Talk to her quick. And be macho about it. Say things like you hear super-masculine movie stars say. Be gruff, burly, and mean. If you're able to grow any beard, definitely let it grow out for four or five days. Come on strong. Strut a lot and act as if you are God's gift to women. She'll love you, and you won't even have to worry about being turned down. Whatever you do, don't be yourself.

Your friend,
Hal

So what do you think? Oh, I know. Hal is a bit obvious, but you have to admit that people do follow advice as bad as his. Kids play vicious games with their parents. Athletes care more about themselves than their team. And senior high guys try to win girls with struts and stunts that would make Hal smile. And they all believe it's the right thing to do!

It's amazing what we'll believe sometimes, isn't it? People peddle truth today like vendors sell candy bars and ice-cream cones. They put it in a nice wrapper, give it a good name, make it taste good, and pin a price on it; and people buy it—even if it isn't good for them.

People spend good money to buy so-called newspapers that are full of lies and gossip. They're desperate enough for truth to call in to a radio psychologist and hang their hopes and dreams on what the person tells them in two minutes over the air.

I'm convinced that many, if not most, of the problems in my life—and maybe in yours—are caused by our choosing to believe what's not true about us, about others, or about God. Here are some untruths I have actually believed at one time or another in my life:

I am a failure, and everybody knows it.

God is out to get me.

I will never, ever get out of this.

I will never, ever get over this.

Nobody will ever want to marry me.

Everyone has to like everything about me.

I look at that little list now, and I laugh, but I wasn't laughing when I believed each item on the list. My misplaced belief left me in pretty bad shape more than once.

So how do you know what's true? It's funny we Christians should ask that. Pontius Pilate once asked the question, "What is truth?" (John 18:38). Somehow no one had gotten the word to him that standing right before his eyes was the very Son of God, who had just the night before said to His disciples, "I am . . . the Truth" (John 14:6). Pilate had the Truth about everything and everyone, the Truth about life and about death, right in front of him, and he missed it.

You have the same truth in front of you. Jesus is the Truth. He says to you, "If you continue in My Word, you are truly My disciples, and you will know the truth, and the truth will make you free" (John 8:31—32).

If you want to know the truth, not Hal's kind of truth, but real truth, the kind that can shape your life into what you're really meant to be, let me suggest these steps:

1. Get close to Jesus. Become a disciple. Learn from what He said and from how He lived.

2. Read the Scriptures. Jesus once prayed, "Sanctify them in the

truth; Thy Word is truth (John 17:17). He had every disciple in mind when He said that prayer—including you. You have to read the Scriptures as more than a duty, though, and as more than an assignment or a chore. Read the Word of God as a seeker of truth, as a miner of precious gems imbedded in the words inspired by God.

3. Test the spirits. God tells us in 1 John 4:1, "Beloved, do not believe every spirit, but test the spirits to see whether they are of God; for many false prophets have gone out into the world." In other words, there are a lot of Hals out there. Test everything you've learned from your Lord in His Word.

4. Pray for knowledge, understanding, and wisdom. Take a moment to read Paul's urging to prayer in Col. 1:9. One of the best reasons to pray is that in response to prayer God molds us into His will. And God's will is always true!

5. Finally, lean on those few, special people in your circle of family and friends who know both God's Word and you. They can help you put the two together. In my own circle of family and friends, I have three people to whom I go when I have a big decision to make or when I'm testing the spirits. These are people who know and love the Lord and me too. They seem to be able to cut through the alternatives with me and help me find the truth. Two of the three people are over 70 years old. One is not. She's my wife. By the way, Hal is not on my list. I hope he's not on yours either.

Q *If God is everywhere, why do I have to worship Him in church?*

A Probably almost everybody would look at the house I grew up in and say it wasn't much. I have to admit that it wasn't plush, fancy, big, or impressive. It was a row house built right up next to the house next door. It was an old house, built in the 1890s, and there were probably, at any one time, seven or eight things not working right in it.

Last summer, though, I visited the old neighborhood, and I found out how much that old red-brick house means to me. You can probably guess, I'm not talking about architecture here or quality or beauty. In all three categories, I'm afraid, the house wouldn't make honorable mention. The reason I loved and still love that house was because of what happened there and because of who was there with me in that house.

Great things happened in that house—great at least as far as my own life story goes: pillow fights, my dad laughing so hard he fell off his chair at the kitchen table, hymn sings after supper on Sunday night, Christmas dinners, Mom caring for Dad when he got so sick. It was all a part of our family, and it all happened in that old house.

I learned what being a good neighbor meant by living in that house. We used to lend items to the next-door neighbor by opening our kitchen window and handing the items across into their kitchen window. I learned about being family in that house and how important commitment is, and hugs, and being a brother, and being a father. When I was a junior in high school, we moved out of that house into the suburbs, but for me that house will always be home because of the love and family spirit I knew there.

I know. This is starting to sound a little bit like the old Waltons TV series. I have a point to make, though. When people share a common tie, when they live together, love each other, dream the same dreams, and hold on to the same hopes, the place where it happens becomes holy.

Did I surprise you by using the word *holy?* I bet I did. You usually think of holy as meaning pure, righteous, clean, and perfect. Let me tell you, our house wasn't holy in that sense. I mean holy the way the Bible often uses the word—as set apart for God's special purposes, as special because God does great things there.

Our home was holy in that sense, and so is your church. Way back, in Old Testament times, God's people began seeing places as special because of what God did there. A place called Bethel (that means "house of God") is an example. So are the tabernacle and the temple. Places became holy because God did marvelous things there, and people came together to receive His love and watch Him at work.

Now, I know, sometimes your church seems anything but holy. People sleep in church. Some even snore until they catch an elbow in the ribs. Kids play hide and seek in the chancel. Guys ogle girls across the aisle. Pastors get mixed up. Bible classes get boring. People gossip about each other right outside the church doors. People whisper about the woman in the mink stole right inside the church doors. People argue at church council meetings, and the services may seem too long.

Still, your church is holy. God does great things there. He gets His Word through to people. He brings babies into His family through Baptism. He forgives sins, offering strength for life in the Lord's Supper. The Lord is busy in your church. He's busy with a group of people who, like my family, may not always have it right and perfect, but who share a common faith, and hope, and love. And that makes your church holy.

What I hope you can see is that you worship your Lord in church not because you have to but because there with those people in that place, you've found a family and a home for worship. Sure, you can worship your Lord all over the place. I say some of my deepest prayers in the shower. I've sung songs of praise as a terrible soloist with an audience of a thousand fir trees in the national forest. (They can't complain.) Sitting on the steps of my old home last summer, I whispered a prayer there, too.

From the start, though, Christians recognized that they needed a group of people to support them, to build them up, and keep them alive in their faith. The Lord's Prayer is full of "our," "us," and "we." It's a prayer for church families more than for individuals going it on their own. Christians really do need each other. Keeping faith alive and active is too difficult on your own. It's like trying to start an outdoor barbecue with one charcoal. Lots of luck! I hope you like raw hamburger!

I'll be real straight with you. The people I know who have tried to be Christians on their own without the support of a church family have not done very well. Often they'll say, "I can worship God where and when I please, and I don't have to go to church to do it." They may mean well, but they end up not doing much worshiping at all.

One of the real problems people your age face is that very often the church doesn't make you feel a part of the family. You're told that you're the church of the future when you have every right to want to be the church now. Adults in churches often don't think about asking youth to be a part of the ministries of the church. No wonder a lot of youth get turned off and wonder, like you, if worshiping and serving the Lord might happen better elsewhere.

I want to leave you with a challenge. I'd like you to promise yourself that over the next four Sundays you'll take on a personal "Back into the Church Family" program. It's meant to help you start feeling more at home in your church. From your question, I think this may be helpful. You have to agree to do it all, though, the whole program. No fudging. You may even ask someone close to you to help you make sure you follow the steps.

So here it is, your "Back into the Church Family" program:
1. Attend church each of the next four Sundays, no matter how you feel in the morning, no matter how many excuses you can give for not going.
2. While attending church each Sunday, write down on the bulletin or on a scrap of paper one important thing you learned during worship.
3. After worship each Sunday, try to answer these questions, seeing how it goes Sunday by Sunday:
   • What good thing happened to me in church today?
   • Whom do I really value at church? Whose friendship and support mean much to me?
4. While at church each Sunday, make a point of talking to at

least one new person. Try to foster some new relationships. It may take work, but you can find a few new friends.

5. Over the next month, try each week to be present at some event at your church other than the Sunday worship service.
6. At the end of the month, think about evaluating the whole experience with your pastor or youth counselor.

The "Back into Your Church Family" program is meant to help you reaffirm how much you need your church family and how much you have to give them. I hope that in 20 years you'll be able to visit your church and have it feel like the holy house it is.

Q *What is the proper way to tell about my faith without sounding too pushy?*

A Have you ever been stopped at a shopping mall or at an airport by someone who wanted to preach to you? I have. Just last week, in fact, a guy stopped me at an airport. He put a Bible right between my eyes and said, "Say, Sir, do you know you're going to hell?" That was what he said. I said, "No, I'm on my way to Chicago." He said, "I think you're going to hell."

Now that guy had no idea who I was. He certainly had no idea that I am a Christian who has received Christ as my personal Savior and Lord. He also didn't know that underneath my topcoat I was wearing a clerical collar. Wow, was I tempted to take off my scarf and with a dramatic move reveal that the man he said was going to hell was actually a Christian pastor. I didn't. Instead, I listened for about 30 seconds.

It turns out that what the guy wanted was to sell me a book about hell, damnation, and the end of the world. He didn't. I went to Chicago. I'm afraid he may think I'm still on my way to hell.

The problem with that guy's approach to telling others about his faith is that he doesn't really know his audience. He had no idea who I was or what I needed or what I felt inside about anything. What's worse, the guy in the airport shoving Bibles into people's faces doesn't tell good news (which is what evangelism really is) but bad news. He isn't offering the gift of salvation but, instead, he's selling something. He's pushy, unlikable, and, frankly, a bad representative of our Lord's compassion and love for everyone. You can tell—I'm not a fan of his at all.

Let me tell you about a better way. The better way to tell others about your faith involves telling three stories. That's right, three stories. The three stories you have to tell are these:

YOUR STORY
MY STORY
HIS STORY

First, you need to tell your story, that is, the story of a friend whom you know and care about. In others words, to be a good communicator of the Christian faith, you need to know your audience. Everyone has their own story. By that I mean that everyone has their own set of needs, dreams, hopes, problems, and struggles.

The best Christian communicators know the person with whom they're talking. If you want to talk about your faith, think about talking one on one. Very few Christians ever have the chance to talk to large groups. Most of us, though, can share our faith with people one at a time.

Before you even begin to say a word to a friend about your faith, ask some very important questions like these:
What does this person need right now in his or her life?
Is this person hurting in any way?
- With what in life is this person struggling?
- Is this person lonely? afraid? worried? depressed?
- How does this person feel about God? about Christ?
- How does this person feel about the church?
- How does this person feel about me?

That's what I mean by getting to know the story of a friend. The Gospel of our Lord and Savior meets a whole supermarket of needs and problems. The greatest challenge in communicating your faith is to make it real for your friend. If you've ever sat through a sermon with the pastor talking about something you couldn't understand or didn't care about, you know what I mean.

Do you know what this means? To be a good Gospel communicator, you have to be a good listener. You have to wait for the door to open. For instance, when a friend says, "It seems like nobody cares anymore," the door has opened. You've heard a need—loneliness. Let the Gospel speak to the need. That's the first story, the story of a friend.

The second story is your own story and ple-e-ease, I don't mean every minute of your life from the sentence "I was born in a hospital because I wanted to be near my mother." What's important is that part of your life that overlaps with your friend's needs and struggles. So, if it's loneliness a friend feels, tell of a time when you were lonely. If it's nervousness over something coming up, think back to a time when you were nervous. Identify with your friend's hurt or problem. Show that you care and that you understand.

Be careful here, though. When telling you own story, be sure not to set yourself up as a super-saint. Make sure, too, that you don't talk so much about yourself that you forget about your friend! Another caution: don't try too hard. I heard about a woman who was trying to console a friend who had lost a husband. Her trying too hard led her to say, "I know just how you feel. My dog died six years ago." Yuck!

It may be that listening, showing that you care, is the best thing you can do. I have a friend who has a way of making me feel special every time we talk. She has a way of zooming in on me. She's this way with whomever she talks to. She's a great listener. She makes people feel that, right now in the world, they are most important. Everything else can wait.

When you tell your own story, as you talk about your faith, the best parts of your story will be those times when you were touched by God. That means that if you want to be a good communicator of your faith, you have to know your life story as a Christian. Call it your holy history, the story of God's acts in your life. Be sure to take time to get to know your highs and lows over the years, spiritually.

That leads me to the third and most important story you tell—His story, the story of Christ. His life, death, and resurrection all offer specific good news for specific problems. Is your friend lonely? Talk about how Jesus was lonely once, too. Talk about His loneliness on the cross. Talk about how Jesus promises to be with us always. Best yet, talk about how you, personally, have experienced the love and companionship of Jesus when you were lonely.

See how it works? You find in the life, words, and actions of Jesus the Good News that fits just what your friend needs and at the same time has been your own experience.

The three stories, you see, intersect. In that area where all three stories have a common experience, you've found the most effective and most real communication of your faith.

One more thing about communicating your faith. The language of faith takes practice. It's like learning a second language.

If you want to learn German, for example, there is no better way than to speak it every day. You learn it by doing it. It's the same way with communicating the faith. You need practice.

So the question is: when does practice start? I hope it starts for you soon. Be patient. Be ready. Be gentle. Show respect for your friends, for God's action in your own life, and for the greatest story ever told. You'll know when the time is right, and the words you need will be there.

I'd like to be there to hear you.

If my life has a purpose, what is it?

 You won't believe what I saw the other day. Of all places, I saw it on a table at a garage sale. I'm not sure what to call it. I'm not sure it even has a name. It worked, though. Well, sort of.

It's a metal box with a trapdoor on the top, an off-on switch on the side, and a battery inside to make it work. Not sparing any expense, the garage sale host had put a battery in it so it would work. Anyway, here's what happened. I picked up the little box and turned the switch on. Then a little plastic arm came out of the trapdoor on top of the box, reached to the side of the box, turned the switch off, and then returned inside the box, the trapdoor closing on top of it. That was it. Really.

We've finally done it! We've invented something that has only one purpose—to turn itself off. No wonder it landed at a garage sale. The guy there wanted $3 for it. He can have it. I have a feeling he may have a few hundred more of these little gadgets in a box somewhere. I'm tempted to say, "What a turnoff!" but I won't.

Life is a turnoff sometimes. I don't mean that sometimes we get down. Everybody gets down on things. I mean that for some people life doesn't have much meaning to it beyond just living and finally dying.

Last winter I lost control of my car on the ice. I'm from Minnesota, and I've always considered myself a fairly skilled driver. This time, though, I hit what we call in Minnesota "black ice," and my car just kept sliding. I couldn't do a thing about it. The car was going its own direction, and I wasn't steering it. Putting on the brakes wouldn't help either. In fact, whatever I did didn't seem to work. The car was out of control, and it stayed out of control until I landed in a ditch.

Just maybe the way I felt driving that car is the way you feel about your life sometimes. Where is it going? Why am I here? Where am I headed? You see, not having a purpose in life means not having direction either. You've asked a very good question. It may be one of the most important questions anybody can ever ask.

I want you to know right off that, yes, life does have a purpose to it. When God, the Creator of all life, made the first human beings, He made them in His image (Gen. 1:26–27). That meant that people had souls and minds and hearts that could be given to God. Just as important, though, being made in God's image meant that human beings were designed to reflect what God is like—to be like Him, as much as any creature can be like its Creator.

You know what happened next. Adam and Eve sinned, and, in the process, they presented a much-less-than-perfect image of God. They weren't chips off the old block anymore. That's for sure.

Still, the original purpose of God in making human beings in His image stands. We're still meant to reflect God's nature. We're meant to bring Him glory. That really means that we're meant to show people in what we do and what we say how God is, what He's like, and the kinds of things God does.

If you wonder how that sort of purpose to life works out, the best Person to watch is Jesus. Col. 1:15 actually calls Him "the image of the invisible God." In Jesus, our heavenly Father has shown us all exactly what He's like. He's shown us, too, what the purpose of our lives is.

I have an uncle whom I greatly admired as a child. Truth is, I still admire him. As a child, though, I loved and respected him so much that I wanted to be just like him. I tried to walk like him, talk like him, even laugh like him. He was and still is one of the kindest, most gracious people I've ever met. There is no greater compliment anyone could ever give me than to say, "You know, you remind me a lot of your Uncle Bill." No greater compliment except for one, "You know, what you did there, what you said, it was very Christlike."

So the purpose of our lives as Christians is to glorify God. That means we're meant to show others what God is like. There is no better way to do that than to try to be like Christ. Maybe that's what Paul meant when he said, "For to me to live is Christ" (Phil. 1:21).

The Presbyterians have a catechism called *The Westminster Catechism*. One of the questions asked in their catechism is "What is the purpose of life?" I just love the answer they give. Are you ready?

The purpose of human life is to love and serve God and enjoy Him forever.

Isn't that great? It pretty much says it all. The purpose of your life is all tied up with God. You're meant to love Him, serve Him, and enjoy Him forever!

Now I want to tell you something. It's one of the best kept secrets around. This is too bad, but it's true. The secret is this: the more you fulfill your life's purpose of glorifying God, the happier and the more satisfied you'll be.

And let me give you another one, too: the more you reflect what God is like, as you've come to know Him in the Bible and in Jesus Christ, the happier and more satisfied you'll be.

I think that's why we feel so fulfilled and content and rich and happy when we create something—because God is creative, and we're meant to reflect His image. It's why we feel great when we love—because God is love, and we're meant to reflect His image. Doing the right thing, making sacrifices, giving—they all bring us fulfillment inside because they all have us reflecting just how God is.

Do you see how this begins to work out? Once you know what your overall purpose in life is (to love, serve, and enjoy God forever), then you begin to get some direction in life. Suddenly, some things you thought were important aren't all that big in your life. And maybe some things that used to be unimportant now seem at the center of it all.

The trick is to find how you can best fulfill this purpose. All kinds of secondary life purposes are out there. They're all meant to help you bring God glory. Here are some examples:

helping the hurting	being creative
bringing joy to others	building
teaching	telling about God
learning	encouraging

The best thing to do while you are young is to find your

horse and ride it out. Try a lot of things. Don't settle in right away. Look for things that bring you fulfillment and an inner peace. Listen to how people respond when you've tried your hand at some new venture. But when you find what you do well and what at the same time gives you a great opportunity to show others what God and His people are like, go for it. Climb on that horse and ride him out. He's yours. You'll find he rides much better than a car on Minnesota black ice.

Q

Why do people criticize and degrade others?

A

I remember him well. We never called him by his real name. We made up a name. It was easier that way. He looked different. He walked with a limp. The girls didn't want to dance with him in P.E. class. We did imitations of him. He usually sat alone in the cafeteria. Then something happened.

A teacher got up in an assembly one morning and announced that this very same guy would now play the piano. We snickered. There were hoots and whistles and cackles as he limped over to the piano. Nobody expected much. We were sure it was just charity. Someone felt sorry for him.

Then he played. My, did he play. The piano sang. He made the keys dance. One foot was on the peddle, his bad one, and the other, well, it bounced and boogied with the music. It was as if he came alive behind the piano. He smiled, and we had never seen him smile before. You could tell. He was home. Behind that piano was where he was meant to be.

When he finished playing, there was this silence. We all seemed to realize at that moment that we had never really seen this guy or known him. He finished by playing "Beautiful Savior," of all things. I still remember it. Wow, was it something to hear!

Then, after the silence, we applauded. We stood up, and we applauded. He simply got up from the piano and went back to his place in the bleachers. I think he didn't trust our applause. I don't blame him either. We kept applauding, though, and he finally stood and waved. The assembly ended.

From that day on, though, I never saw him in the same way. No one else did either. He played often after that. At a spring concert, he played a piano solo that brought everyone to their feet. He accompanied our singing in school chapel services. Today I can't sing "Beautiful Savior" without thinking of him.

Looking back, I can see how much the Lord taught me in that experience. For one thing, I understand now why we gave this classmate such a hard time. Here are some of the reasons: He was different and didn't meet our standards.

We assumed that he had no gifts worth celebrating.
We all fell in line and followed the crowd when it came to re-
sponding to him.

Another reason for our degrading of this gifted person is more
difficult to admit. I believe I put him down because, in putting him
down, I somehow thought my own stature was raised. I think you
know what I mean. We often criticize others because it makes us
feel superior, better, more popular, and accepted. As I said, it isn't
easy to admit, but sometimes I have attempted to make myself
look good by making others look bad. It's a nasty game and certainly runs against how we Christians are meant to relate to others, but it was there. I admit it.

The Lord knows this side of me—and of you. In the Bible He
makes clear that even Christians can say things that curse and de-
grade others. Take, for example, James 3:8–10:

> But no human being can tame the tongue—a restless evil, full
> of deadly poison. With it we bless the Lord and Father, and
> with it we curse men, who are made in the likeness of God.
> From the same mouth come blessing and cursing. My breth-
> ren, this ought not to be so.

No wonder a woman once described the Bible as "the book
that reads me!" Putting people down, mocking them, laughing at
them behind their backs, it's all a part of our ugly sinful side. As
James wrote, considering God's love for us and His love for all
people, "this ought not be so." We're designed by the Holy Spirit
to be people who always seek the highest good in others, who
love them and speak well of them no matter what. That's how
God treats us. That's how we're meant to treat others.

I want you to think right now about one person who is often
the object of criticism and put-downs. Think about someone who
has no friends at school. Picture this person in your mind. What
about this person is different or unique? Why do you think he or
she is given such a hard time by others? What traits of this person
are often singled out for ridicule or criticism? Got the picture?
Spend a few minutes trying to answer to yourself some of these
questions. Let's make what we say here as real as possible. Don't

read on until you've pictured this person in your mind and thought about the question I've raised.

Good, now I want to help you help another person "made in the likeness of God." I want you, as you read each of the statements below, to insert this person's name in the appropriate place. Each statement points the way to putting a stop to some nasty business. Here goes.

1. *Name* is someone created in God's image and loved to death by Jesus Christ.
2. *Name* is, therefore, worthy of my respect and love.
3. I will pray for *Name*, asking the Lord to provide me strength and to help me find and affirm *Name's* gifts.
4. I will actively watch for *Name* to display his or her strengths and gifts, and when I see them, I will celebrate them out loud with compliments.
5. I will not attempt to make myself look good by joining others in putting *Name* down. I will stand apart. When others curse *Name*, I will bless him or her.
6. When I hear others ridicule *Name*, I will choose one or more of these strategies:
   a. I will walk away.
   b. I will say that I'd just as soon not hear that sort of talk.
   c. I will say something positive about *Name*.
   d. I will ask those ridiculing *Name* to consider why they do it.
7. I will break the barrier that ridicule has put between *Name* and myself and give *Name* the gift of my time and my kindness.

Commitments like these ask a lot of us, but then Jesus often asks a lot of us. He never said we could just join the crowd and do what it does. He never settled for that Himself. He was always taking the side of those who were different and outcast.

He lived with a lot of mockery. He died an outcast Himself. I think of that often—especially when I sing "Beautiful Savior."

Q *Why do I give in when temptation comes?*
Why do I keep doing what's wrong?

A Let's begin by talking about chocolate chip cookies. I
know that chocolate chip cookies don't seem to be very
theological to you, but they are to me. Here's why.
I love chocolate chip cookies. We're talking love. I especially love
the soft kind, fresh out of the oven. Maybe you do, too.

I have a problem, though. In fact, I have two problems when
it comes to eating chocolate chip cookies. For one thing, I'm gain-
ing weight fast, and if I don't quit eating so much soon, someone
might mistake me for the Goodyear blimp or at least a close rela-
tive. I know overeating isn't good for me—and that includes overeating chocolate chip cookies. Now here's the second problem: I
can't stop eating chocolate chip cookies once I start. I get carried
away. I eat and eat until I'm stuffed.

You might say I have a weakness for chocolate chip cookies.
A love becomes a weakness, you see, because cookies promise
me pleasure but, in the long run, deliver me pain.

Temptation is like that. Temptation promises people pleasure
or gain as it draws them closer and closer to evil. It can be chocolate chip cookies on the lighter side, but on the heavier side it can
be a temptation to steal or to lie or to cheat. We're tempted because we think we'll be happier or richer on the other end. What
really happens, though, is we end up sadder and poorer because
we've given in again. We've made a compromise with the devil.
We've lost, spiritually speaking. As long as we're Christian, that
will bother us.

I'd like to help you in your desire to come up a winner in
your struggle against temptation. First, though, you need your pri-
mary weapon—God's Word. Get a Bible, if one is nearby, and
we'll mine the Word for strategies for winning over temptation.
Don't read on until you've got your hands on a Bible.

OK.

Strategy No. 1. **Get to know how temptation works.** In
your Bible turn to James 1:13–15. These three verses tell us a lot
about temptation. Here are some of the truths we learn:

1. God does not tempt us (v. 13, "He Himself tempts no one"). God may create chocolate chip cookies, but it's the devil and the sin within me that make me want to eat too much and jeopardize my health.
2. When the devil tempts us, he presents us with just what arouses us. He knows our weakness, and he'll go after it. He goes for us, one by one. We each face our own distinctive set of temptations (v. 14, "but each person is tempted . . . by his own desire").
3. Temptation always has bad consequences at the other end. Verse 15 talks about desire leading to sin, and sin leading to death. Each temptation has its own bad ending—unless we overcome it as spiritual winners.

Strategy No. 1 asks you to stop and take an inventory. Where are your weak points? Where does sin keeping happening in your life? Where do you usually wage your battles against Satan?

This strategy also asks you to take time in the midst of a temptation to weigh carefully the consequences of your decision. At their best, Christians are able to cut through the promises of pleasure and gain to see the bad results of a sinful decision. Lately, when I get a craving for a dozen chocolate chip cookies, I imagine myself stepping on our digital bathroom scale and blowing the thing up with my weight. Guess what? It works.

Strategy No. 2. **Avoid situations and people that make it easier for you to give in to temptation.** If you'd like to read a just-about "Rated R" story of one person's ability to do this, read about Joseph and Potiphar's wife in Gen. 38:6b–18. Note how in verses 8–9 Joseph carefully weighs the consequences of yielding to this temptation. He puts Strategy No. 1 to work. When Mrs. Potiphar continues, though, look at what he does in verse 12. Joseph knew that he was in a compromising situation and with a person that made it very easy to yield to temptation. So he did the right thing. He left the situation and the person behind.

Ps. 1:1 promises happiness to the person who doesn't "walk in the counsel of the ungodly." The company we keep definitely

affects our ability to overcome temptation. That leads to Strategy No. 3.

Strategy No. 3. **Surround yourself with people who know God's Word, who share your loyalty to Christ, and who know you inside and out.** This doesn't mean you become a monk in the desert. It means you have people who build you up and help you grow as a Christian. It also means you can go to these people in times of temptation for guidance and strength.

Strategy No. 4. **Pray.** Jesus once said, "Watch and pray that you may not enter into temptation" (Matt. 26:41). To pray is to tap the power that has already defeated Satan. Prayer grabs hold of the hand of God in temptation. It fills a mind thinking evil with thoughts of God and His power.

Strategy No. 5. **Guard your intake.** In other words, watch what you allow to become a part of you. What goes in comes out sooner or later. Garbage in garbage out. Seeds of subtle temptation get planted that grow into crops of evil. Good Christians are good farmers. Phil. 4:8–9 provides some good advice on what to fill up on. Unfortunately, chocolate chip cookies are not on Paul's list.

Strategy No. 6. **Arm yourself with the Word of God.** Of all the strategies, this is the most important one. When Jesus faced His temptation in the desert, He used God's Word as a weapon against Satan (cf. Matt. 4:1–11).

In Eph. 6:10–20, we're given an inventory of the spiritual armor we need in our battles with the devil. Look carefully at the list. You'll find only one offensive weapon. The rest are all defensive. The one offensive weapon that sends the devil running (v. 17) is the sword of the Spirit, the Word of God.

The Word of God works against the devil. David knew that. He knew about temptation (remember Bathsheba?), but he also knew that the Word of God was what he needed to overcome temptation. In Ps. 119:11, he wrote, "I have laid up Thy word in my heart, that I might not sin against Thee."

Want to have the best tool there is when temptation comes? Memorize the Scriptures. Put the Word of God "in your heart" so that when temptation strikes, it's there, ready to be driven right into Satan.

I can think of no better advice to someone facing an ongoing temptation than to begin studying and putting to memory the Word of God. It will mean a little time each day. Memorize just a little bit each day, but memorize it well. You'll be armed for the battle.

Strategy No. 7. **In temptation, trust the promises of God.** In 1 Cor. 10:13 the Lord makes a great promise to any Christian facing temptation. Read it, believing that the "you" in this verse *is* you. No matter what temptation you face, God will provide a way out. That's a promise. You can count on it.

I hope this helps. Oh, oh. More important, I hope all of this helps me because I'm in my study at home right now, and I have this certain craving for you know what.

Q *Why bother praying to if God has everything all figured out anyway?*

A Something tells me that you and your Lord are not on such good terms. I don't mean that in a judgmental way. I only mean that when we stop talking to someone—or think about cutting off communication—we're usually not on the best of terms. What's true of our relationship with other people is true of our relationship with God. Talking with God in prayer is a sign of a healthy relationship. Not talking to Him or wondering if it's worthwhile are signs of a possibly weakening relationship.

It happens often in friendships—this breakdown in talk. For all kinds of reasons, friends may begin to talk less with each other. They find new friends. They find new interests not shared between each other. They may move away from each other, and the distance may make talk difficult or expensive. So they talk less, and the less they talk, the weaker their friendship becomes.

I know the same thing happens in marriages. A couple begins to grow apart. Each spouse chases a separate set of goals. They pass each other on the way. Then suddenly, one of them realizes what's happening and says across the kitchen table, "We've got to do something. We're just not talking anymore." So they do something. If they're smart, they do something. They see a counselor or their pastor. They begin talking again, and the more they talk, the stronger their marriage becomes.

What I'm trying to tell you is this: *yes, we pray to God to make things happen in our lives, to change things, but we pray for many other reasons, too.* Let me show you what I mean.

First, **prayer teaches us dependency.** When we pray, we realize that we can't do life as a soloist. We are dependent on God. We need Him. We rely on Him. As I look at the times in my own life when I've prayed very little, I see times when I was trying to live life on my own. Prayer teaches us humility. That's why praying on your knees is a good idea. I recommend it. The more we pray, the more God is recognized as our Provider and Lord.

Second, **prayer is one way by which God gets us in**

tune with His will. I know a teenager, for instance, who was very sick with a rare form of cancer. He faced lots of therapy and several operations. When he first heard about the cancer, his prayers always went something like this:

Lord, take this cancer away from me. Heal me. Send a miracle. Save me from death.

Not a bad prayer. As months passed, though, this boy's faith grew and grew. He found himself trusting and loving his Lord more than he ever had before the cancer was discovered. I remember being with him late one night when he added this prayer to the one I had spoken at his bedside:

Lord, if it's not Your will to heal me of this cancer, then give the faith and the patience to make it through what's ahead.

Gradually, you see, the Lord had led this courageous Christian to place himself in his Father's arms and trust that what he needed the Lord would give. Through the Lord's response to his prayer he had learned to face his disease and his future with confidence.

A third reason we pray is that **through prayer we exercise an expensive privilege.** When we pray, we talk to the Lord of the Universe, the Creator of everything and everyone that ever was or will be. That's no small talk!

To illustrate this, let me share one of my wildest dreams with you. I actually dreamed this a few years ago. I remember it as vividly as if it happened last night. In my dream I was kneeling by my bedside praying. Suddenly an angel appeared right there in my room. Don't ask me why my wife didn't wake up. Dreams aren't always that tight, you know.

Anyway, this bright and shining angel stopped me right in the middle of Luther's evening prayer and said, "Excuse me." Naturally, I was willing to excuse him or her or whatever pronoun you use for an angel.

"Yes?" I said. "What can I do for you?" I wondered if the angel had gotten lost or was looking for a place to stay.

"You, Sir," the angel said, "are addressing the Most High

and Holy Lord of Lords. You are talking to Yahweh, to the great I AM!"

"Yes, I am," I told the angel. "I talk to Him every night about this time."

Suddenly the angel got a frightening, awesome look on his face. He grew brighter, it seemed. Then he reached toward me and pointed his finger at me and said, "By what right do you talk to the Lord? Who do you think you are to address the Almighty?" Now both of his index fingers pointed to me as he bellowed in the night, "Tell me, and tell me now. What makes you think you may have an audience with God?!"

Then guess what happened. Right. I woke up.

If I ever get another chance at that dream, though, I know exactly what I'd say to that angel. I'd say, "So you want to know what right I have to talk to God. My right to prayer was purchased and won for me by Jesus Christ. He died so that I could have these moments with the Father. That's why I close every prayer with the words 'in the name of Jesus.' " If I was really on a roll with my friend the angel I'd even quote Eph. 3:11–12 and Heb. 4:14–16.

One of the reasons Jesus died was to open for us a line of communication with the Father. Prayer comes with an expensive price tag. It's a privilege that doesn't come cheap. To take it for granted or to say it's a bother is to cheapen the sacrifice our Savior made to get us through to God.

All three of the reasons I've listed for prayer have one thing in common: each is tied up with our relationship with God. Prayer puts into words our dependency on God, our desire to do His will, and our gratitude for the expensive privilege of being on speaking terms with the Lord Himself.

If God never once gave us exactly what we asked in prayer, those three reasons would stand. They'd be reason enough to keep on praying. Truth is, though, God does answer prayer in His own time and in His own way. Sure, He sees the broad picture, and, sure, He knows the end of the story. That's no reason to stop praying, though. It's another reason to keep praying! Who better to ask than the One who knows?!

The Bible teaches again and again that prayer really does

change things (James 5:16b). The changes may not always match our will, but when we pray, God listens and God acts. His will gets done. Through it all, He keeps moving us ahead toward a good purpose (Rom. 8:28–30).

What more can we ask than that . . . except maybe one more shot at an angel?

Why do people take so much for granted?

 Our church did a very good thing a while back. I'll never forget it. It was called an Awareness Banquet and was sponsored by our Social Ministry Committee. Here's how it worked.

We were all invited to a banquet and were asked to reserve places ahead of time. The cost per plate was to be $5 per person, which we were to pay when we arrived the night of the banquet. All we knew was that it was an Awareness Banquet and that banquets at church are usually tasty and fun.

When we arrived at the door, though, we were met by a host, who told us: Tonight you will become aware of what it is like to be handicapped. Throughout the evening you are to experience the challenge of the handicap described on the slip of paper you receive.

We were each given a slip of paper. On the paper were simple sentences like these: **You are blind. You are paralyzed from the waist down. You are deaf. You are too poor to afford the $5 fee and must wait outside. You are paralyzed from the neck down. You are a starving person on the other side of the world. Go home.**

The list of challenges went on. People were blindfolded. Others had their ears plugged so that they couldn't hear. Others found themselves in wheelchairs. Others went home hungry or had to wait out in the hall until the banquet was over. Still others were asked to care for the handicapped—feeding some, leading others, and helping get the wheelchairs into place.

It was quite a banquet. Afterwards, we all came together to talk about what we had experienced. Even the people who had been sent home came back to church. One common idea was expressed by almost everyone: Wow! Do we take for granted what we have!

I guess you see that. In a way it's good that you see it now while you're still young. Some people get to be 60 or 70 before they see it—how we take so much for granted. They suddenly realize that they've been living life like, well, like a person rollerskating through an art gallery. It can be fun. It goes fast. You get noticed. Along the way, though, you miss the beauty, the fine points, the little things, the simple but special gifts.

Maybe your school has performed a play that makes the point very well. The play is *Our Town*, written way back in 1938 by Thornton Wilder. He won a Pulitzer Prize for the play. *Our Town* celebrates the simple yet rich beauties of life. If in a thousand years someone finds a copy of the play, I think they'll get a pretty true picture of what mattered most in America in 1938 and today, too.

One of Wilder's characters, Emily, dies young in the play. She receives her wish, though, to come back to life and relive a single day from her years on earth. She chooses a day from her childhood. And guess what. Remember? It's all too much for her to take in—the sights, sounds, and smells. She can't handle it. It's too rich, too deep, too wonderful. She wonders out loud if anyone ever realizes the richness of life while they're still living it. As I recall, the Stage Manager answers that maybe just the poets and the saints do, but that's about it.

Chances are, you're not a poet. As a Christian, though, you qualify for sainthood—oh, not the halo variety of sainthood, but true sainthood. To be a saint means that you have been chosen, singled out, and called to be different from the rest of the world. This doesn't mean that you look weird or dress strangely and have people snickering behind your back. It means you're different, spiritually.

One of the most important ways in which you're unique is that, as a Christian saint, you're a beholder. Maybe you never thought of yourself as a beholder, but it's what you're meant to be. Beholders see things others miss. Beholders see God where others would never think of finding Him. Beholders find God all over life—in it, under it, over it, at the beginning of it, and at the end of it. Beholders believe in angels; and in burning bushes; in miracles, great and small; and in life, all of it; as a gift.

This idea of beholding is something we have to work at. Otherwise, we'll end up living life without realizing what we have. You've seen it already:

We take the people we love for granted;
We take our health for granted;
We take our food, clothing, and home for granted;
We take our Lord for granted.
We just live life without beholding it. We race. We rush. We never stop long enough for an inventory. We have a success, but before we can even celebrate it, we're already busy with the next task. We don't take time. We don't say what needs to be said and do what needs to be done until it's often too late.

I have a friend whose mother passed away about a year ago. I told her about your question because I remembered something she had said at her mother's funeral. She told me it was all right for me to repeat her words here for you. This is what she said:

> There were a lot of things I wanted to say to Mom. I wanted to tell her how much I appreciated the hours she spent when I was so sick as a child. I wanted her to know that I am truly grateful for the Christian education I received and for the job she took to send me to college. I had wanted to tell her that I thought she was beautiful and that no one could ever have a better mother. She died, though, before I could tell her. I think she knew. I hope she knew. If I can say anything to you that's important, I want you all to do something: tell your parents that you love them and tell them that today.

There are times in the church, not often, but precious times, when we are very real with each other. Something gets said that everyone recognizes as true and important. The words of this friend brought such a time to our church. She was asking us all to be beholders—to be different in seeing and celebrating life while we live it. She had missed one of her opportunities. She didn't want us to miss ours.

No one gets the chance Emily gets in *Our Town* to relive life. Days are not recyclable. Even Emily finds you can't go back. That means you have now to live life and to behold it. St. Paul called it "making the most of the time" (Eph. 5:16). But then he was a saint, and saints do see things differently from the rest of the world.

136

Q *Why do I have to suffer so much? Is God playing a game with me, or what?*

A You may not know it, but your question ranks right up there with the best questions human beings have ever asked. Great thinkers throughout history have wondered about suffering. In the Bible, Job asks the question over and over again.

The problem comes because we want to believe in a kind and loving Lord, who wills the best for us. If that's true, though, that we have a Lord who loves us, why would He allow us to suffer? How can a good God permit such evil in people's lives, especially when the people are His?

Now I know you're looking for more than just a compliment for asking such a good question. You're in the middle of something that has you wondering about your Lord. Does He care? Can you trust Him when He says He loves you? A lot is riding on your question. I understand that.

A man named Elie Wiesel understands how much rides on suffering, too. He is a survivor of the concentration camps in Europe during World War II. You may remember from your history classes that under the Third Reich in Germany nearly six million Jews lost their lives in these camps. Somehow Wiesel survived.

A few year ago I heard Wiesel tell a story from his experience in one of the camps. He tells the same story in his book *Night*. The prisoners in one of the camps, Wiesel among them, were all brought into the central area of the camp. There they were forced to look on as a 10-year-old boy was hanged in front of them. As the prisoners watched the horror, Wiesel heard a voice in the crowd asking, "Where is God in this?" No answer came. Again, the question, "Where is God?"

Finally, Weisel answered, "God is there. God is hanging there." For Wiesel, at that point, the shock and the suffering had become so great, that for him, God died with that boy on the gallows. As a Jew, Wiesel would later believe again in God, but in that moment of deep pain, he had lost his faith in a God of love.

A lot rides on your question.

One of the best things about the Bible is that it's real. By that I mean that the Bible is true to life. In the Bible, people suffer. In the Bible, even God's Son suffers. In fact, Jesus' suffering is right there near the center of the Christian message. It's through Jesus' suffering and death that God makes things right between us and Him.

I think the Gospel holds the clue to answering your question. Here's the clue:

Through suffering, God achieves *good* purposes.

Just as the suffering of Jesus was for a good purpose, your suffering, too, is meant for good.

Why do you, a Christian, have to suffer? The Bible doesn't offer just one answer, but several. Each answer shows in its own way how God can use something so terribly bad as suffering for a good purpose. I want to list no less than 15 answers to your question from the Bible. You may want to get your Bible out and read each of the passages listed. Take time with each of the principles. Read the passage(s) for each. Think them through. Pray them through. Circle the principles that may be at work in your suffering now. Ready?

1. Through suffering God gets our attention and teaches us. Without suffering, we may try to live life without God and learn little. (Job 36:15)
2. Through suffering we may come to understand God better — His power and His love. I hope this is happening for you right now. (Job 42:3)
3. Through suffering we learn endurance and steadfastness. (Rom. 5:3–5; James 1:2–3)
4. Through suffering God's good purposes in our lives are achieved. (Rom. 8:28)
5. Through suffering we become more Christlike. (Rom. 8:29)
6. Through suffering we are equipped to comfort others who suffer. (2 Cor. 1:4)
7. Through suffering we learn that we are dependent. We learn to rely on God. (2 Cor. 1:9)
8. Through suffering we are humbled. Without it, we may get

conceited and think we can do fine on our own. (2 Cor.
12:7)

9. Through suffering we can rediscover the strength of the Lord
at work within us. (2 Cor. 12:10)
10. Through suffering we may be receiving a gift of God, that is,
an opportunity. (Phil. 1:29)
11. Through suffering our relationship with the Lord is strength-
ened. (Phil. 3:10)
12. Through suffering we share in Christ's suffering. We know
better what it was like for Him on earth, how He is truly one
with us, even in our sufferings. (Phil. 3:10)
13. Through suffering we learn obedience. In a hard time, we
may actually begin to seek God's will and to do it rather than
go with the crowd. (Rom. 12:1–2; Heb. 5:8)
14. Through suffering the Lord disciplines us and proves His love
for us. We always say we want a God of love. God may have
more love for us than we ever thought! He may love us
enough to put us through hard times for our own good—to
correct us and straighten us out. (Heb. 12:5–11; Rev. 3:19)
15. Through suffering we can witness to God's glory. The blind
man whom Jesus healed became a witness. His blindness was
used to show God's glory! (John 9:1–3)

That's probably more than you really wanted me to give you.
The 15 answers, though, work together to say, *"Through suffering, God achieves good purposes."* God doesn't play games with
suffering. He doesn't get a kick out of putting people through
tough times. God doesn't smile when we hurt. He doesn't zap His
creatures like some celestial video-game player blowing up enemy
invaders.

Whatever your suffering or hard times might be, you need a
plan. Here are a few suggestions:
● Focus in faith on God's goodness, His love for you.
● Pray. Keep those lines of open communication busy. Tell your
Lord where you hurt and how you feel.
● Read the Scriptures. The Bible will confirm for you that your
Lord is kind and full of love.
● Surround yourself with helping friends. Don't go it alone.
● Ask yourself questions like these: How will I grow through this

experience? What is the Lord trying to teach me in this? What good purpose will God achieve in this?

I should tell you—as if you don't already know. It's very unlikely that when a hard time hits, you'll be able to look at the list of 15 answers above and say, "Oh, this is a No. 13!" It doesn't work that way, at least not very often. It takes time to see through a bad situation to the good working underneath it all.

There is good there, though. That's a promise.

Q Why Does My Friend Make Bad Decisions? Why is Lisa moving back with her mom when they don't get along at all?

A I don't know Lisa, and I don't know her mom. This isn't "Dear Abby." So I won't even try to give advice here. Your question, though, really is worth a comment.

On the one hand, your question is a good one. It shows how much you care about Lisa. A real part of Christian friendship and Christian love is seeking the highest good of another person. Obviously, you seek Lisa's highest good.

It isn't easy watching those we care about make decisions that look pretty bad from where we're sitting. It's even worse when one bad decision follows another. Some of us (myself included) can be pretty skilled at stringing together one giant catastrophe. Very often the big crises in our lives are not the result of one big, bad decision but rather the outcome of a whole series of little bad decisions.

Sometimes I wonder what it must be like for God from His celestial point of view to watch us blunder through life. He must really see some bad moves in the game of life. Since He created the game, manufactured it, and made the players, too, He must get pretty upset with us at times.

God is love. That means He seeks the highest good of everyone who's ever lived. His friendship with the world, including you and me, moved Him to sacrifice His Son on our behalf. All this must make it very hard for God up there in His heavenly grandstand, watching us fumble, bumble, and fail.

The feeling you have about Lisa is a feeling that comes with love. That makes it, in one sense, a good feeling. It's one God shares with you. In fact, you may just have this feeling about Lisa's decision because you're designed to be like God.

Now you can probably guess I'm going to come at it from another angle. In another sense, your question about Lisa's decision to return to her mom is dangerous. Here's why. Sometimes being a friend means giving your friend the right to make her own decisions. A vital part of friendship is allowing space for each other to decide, to expand, to grow, and maybe even to fail.

It's fair to second-guess Lisa's decision. It's even fair to tell her about your concerns and to ask your question of her straight out. What's unfair, though, is to try to have Lisa live her life as you'd like her to live it or as you live your own life. You're not Lisa. Being her friend means allowing her to make decisions— even when you may disagree with them.

This idea of providing space is very important not only in friendships but also in families. Sometimes, for instance, parents can so seek the good of their children that they smother them with love. They make all their decisions for them. They pick their clothes, choose their friends, and push them into a vocation. I bet you've met some kids like this. It's really pretty sad.

I know a girl who said that she never spoke a word until she was three years old. She didn't have any sort of physical disability. She simply didn't speak because it wasn't necessary. She got everything she needed without ever saying a word. Her parents and brothers and sisters gave her everything before she could ask for it. I know. It sounds pretty good from where you sit right now, but it wasn't healthy for a three-year-old.

Real love grants distance, even when we have concerns for those we love. Not to grant the distance is to turn our friends into slaves or puppets and ourselves into masters. Sometimes, I'm afraid, the very things we can't stand about parents show up in our own friendships.

Now about Lisa. I'm not sure where she's been living since she left her mom. I'm also not sure why she left. I can make some guesses, though, as to why she'd move back with her mom even though they don't get along. Here are some of those guesses, and they are just that—guesses:

- She may be drawn to Mom because family members are designed by God to be drawn to each other. Family was God's idea. He's programmed us to be part of families. Moms and daughters are meant to be together. Parents and children are meant to be together. Running away or living away from home goes against God's basic will that families stay together.
- Maybe Lisa realizes that an important part of her relationship with her mom is commitment. She may see that even if the

relationship is rocky it's worth trying to hold it together. It may be easier for Lisa to stay away, but maybe she sees that nothing worthwhile comes without cost—even good relationships. It may just be that the hurts Lisa and her mom inflict on each other can't compare with the love that ties them together. I hope so. I'm sure you do, too.

● It could be that Lisa, her mom, or both of them have decided to make the changes necessary to be able to live together again. One of the changes might be deciding to accept each other as they are. Time apart can be a real help in this decision for mutual acceptance.

If I were Lisa's friend, I'd do all I can to stand by her as she moves back with her mom. Here are some specific things I'd say and do:

1. I'd be sure that Lisa's sure that she is in no danger in moving back with her mom. That is, I'd ask her if there is any chance of their fights ever getting violent.
2. I'd tell Lisa that she can count on me.
3. I'd take every chance I get to build up Lisa's relationship with her mom. I'd get to know her mom, to understand her, and to appreciate her good points.
4. I'd pray for specific blessings from the Lord and His Spirit for Lisa and her mom—blessings like the fruit of the Spirit in Gal. 5:22–23.
5. I'd be very honest with Lisa, explaining my concerns about her decision but also pledging my continued friendship and support. In other words, I'd give her the distance she needs and deserves.

One thing your question certainly shows is this: being a friend is not always easy, but it is always rooted in God's kind of love.